DAVID PHARR

THEN CAME SUNDAY

21ST CENTURY CHRISTIAN

Then Came Sunday
ISBN: 978-0-89098-954-8

©2025 by 21st Century Christian, Inc
Nashville, TN 37215
All rights reserved.

Scripture taken from the New King James Version®. Copyright © 1982 by Thomas Nelson. Used by permission. All rights reserved.

Scripture quotations marked (ESV) are from The Holy Bible, English Standard Version® (ESV®), copyright © 2001 by Crossway, a publishing ministry of Good News Publishers. Used by permission. All rights reserved.

Cover design by Jared Kendall

TABLE OF CONTENTS

Preface

Then Came Sunday brings together the sequence of events that pertain to the resurrection of Jesus Christ. It is not "story" in any fictional sense, but actual history based on the biblical record. We believe that on a certain Sunday morning the dead corpse of the man known as Jesus of Nazareth supernaturally came back to life. The narrative is found in the books of Matthew, Mark, Luke, and John, with additional information from other parts of the New Testament.

Our purpose is to encourage familiarity with the Bible record and to understand why Jesus' arising from death is the pivotal event of human history. Most who do not believe in Christ have never considered the complete story with an unbiased and inquisitive mind. We would encourage those who have doubts, or don't agree, to at least know the claims that are made. Christians themselves may tend to be satisfied that the resurrection is true but have not immersed themselves in its various aspects. We may be satisfied to know the end of the story without appreciating the events that led to it. We hope this commentary on the story will both enlighten skeptics and enrich the understanding of believers.

Much of one's interest in any story depends on the reader's visualizing the circumstances and activities. We are far removed from the world of ancient Galilee and Judea, but the story is not about technology. It's about persons, what happened to them and around them, and what they tell about their experiences.

Though the New Testament records (Synoptics and John) differ in various details, they all point to the same conclusion. Their differences are not contradictions. To aid our study, Bible scholars have brought together works that are known as "harmonies," which present the parallel narratives side-by-side. This study blends those accounts in chronological order with commentary and emphasis on their significance. Textual references are available with each sub-section, but for ease of reading, they are not given for every detail. Readers are encouraged to use references to verify the commentary. In some class settings, it may be profitable to read the texts listed with the headings.

Our purpose is to provide material suitable for private reading and reflection as well as for class study. Rather than typical chapter divisions with review questions at the end, there are thought questions after each relatively short section. Students and classes may set their own pace.

Unbelievers deny that Jesus arose from the grave. Atheists claim they know there is no God. Agnostics say it can't be known either way, but practically tend toward denial. Some acknowledge the basic historicity of the resurrection story, but insist that the miraculous elements have alternative explanations. It is important to see how the actual facts do not allow naturalistic theories. This work is not primarily a study on Christian evidences, but does seek to answer certain infidel misrepresentations. The various fields of apologetics (e.g., science, philosophy, archeology) can be helpful, but nothing more certainly establishes the truth of the gospel than Christ's resurrection from the dead. There is no way to prove it except from the Bible story itself.

THEN CAME SUNDAY

CHAPTER ONE

Christ Died for Our Sins

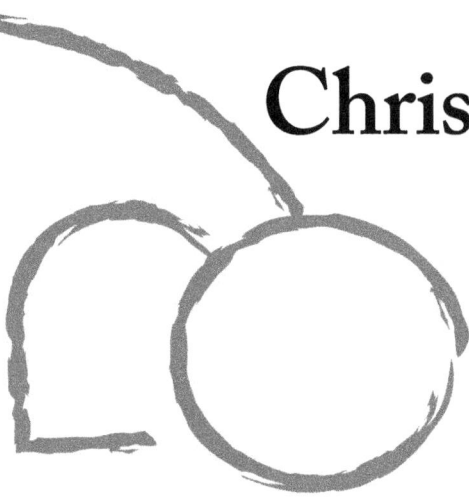

THE CARDINAL FACTS OF THE GOSPEL ARE THAT "CHRIST died for our sins according to the Scriptures, and that He was buried, and that He rose again the third day according to the Scriptures" (1 Corinthians 15:1-4). All else has meaning only because these things are true. This does not discount the importance of all aspects of Jesus' life and ministry. Value is found in all His teaching, as also in His exemplary life, but without His death and resurrection, there would be no basis for believing Him to be the Son of God.

This is history, actual events that occurred in the past. It is not theory, not philosophy, not opinion, but fact. There was a certain man, Jesus of Nazareth, who lived two millennia ago. He was a real man, as actually a real man as any man living today. There was a certain date (whether we know the exact date or not) when He was born, and there was a certain date when He died.

The circumstances and meaning of His death aside, the point to be pressed in the resurrection story is that when He died, He was really dead. Friends took His body, His corpse, and put it into a grave. The lifeless form stayed there through another day, but on the third day, He became alive. The fact that these things occurred a long time ago makes them no less real than if they had happened in our time and were told to us by credible witnesses.

Our faith rests on the historicity of these Gospel facts. Christians believe in facts. Some religions have their foundations in myth, fraud, or philosophy, but Christianity rests on something that actually happened. It is these historical events that give credence to Christianity's doctrines and to the hope it promises. For most of us, persons and events from ancient times seem irrelevant to the modern world. However, the truth of Jesus' death, burial, and resurrection matters for every person who ever lives. Millions may not have heard. Other millions may not believe. Skeptics scoff, agnostics doubt, and most of the world seems indifferent, but Christians believe. Regardless, attitudes and reactions do not alter the facts of history. A man called Jesus once lived. He died. On the third day after His burial, His body came back to life. This all occurred at a specific time and place. If these are not actual facts, they might as well be dismissed and forgotten, and all hope in Christ is a hoax.

On the other hand, if all happened as the Scriptures record, it is of everlasting importance to every soul who ever lives. If indeed Jesus arose, He must be God's Son, the only Savior, and the Lord and Judge of every soul. Ultimately, therefore, all stands or falls on the issue of Christ's bodily resurrection. All New Testament claims for the deity of Jesus and for salvation and hope rest on this truth. Without the resurrection, there would be no gospel and without the gospel, no faith, and without faith, no hope.

Yet many, even many who claim affiliation with Christianity, question or deny its actuality. Theological liberalism believes in the resurrection story only as metaphor, symbolizing the possibility of better things for humanity. Assuming everything supernatural must be doubted, even denied, it is thought impossible that the body of Jesus could have come back to life. It is a strange incongruity that some churches celebrate a tradition of Easter each year, with all their trappings, including cloth-draped crosses and sunrise services, though in many cases, they doubt or deny what the Easter tradition is supposed to represent. There is more to being a Christian than belief in the resurrection, but it is impossible to be a Christian in the original sense without believing He arose.

What are named as the three essential facts of the gospel?

. . . .

How does Christianity's basis in history differ from other religions?

. . . .

What makes the truth or falsity of this history of vital importance?

Naturalistic Explanations

That the man known as Jesus once lived in the Middle Eastern country now called Palestine, no informed person can deny. It is unquestioned history that multitudes of His own generation knew Him. Even ancient non-Christian sources attest that the man Jesus existed (e.g., Jewish Talmud and Roman historians). Some may be so uninterested or uninformed as to flippantly dismiss the entirety of the New Testament records. Other unbelievers, however, as students of history, are forced to admit that the evidence is too abundant to dismiss without an alternative explanation. They know that the New Testament books, in spite of unparalleled critical examination, are the most accredited ancient documents in existence. They accept the parts that He was crucified, was taken down, and buried in a nearby chamber. They know that a short time later, there were reports of the grave being empty, that no corpse was ever found, and that eyewitnesses claimed to have seen Him alive in various circumstances. Among Christians, these facts are evidence of His resurrection. Skeptics suppose, however, that there are other explanations. One hypothesis is that when they buried Jesus, He was not actually dead, only that He appeared to be and that after being left in the grave, He resuscitated and exited the tomb. This so-called "swoon theory" says He had only fallen into a deep coma. After being left alone in the crypt for a while, His mind and strength returned.

A kindred scenario involves a plot with certain of His friends. They had provided a drug that would put Him into a death-like state, but when alone, they used an antidote that caused Him to revive. The purpose of the scheme was to deceive the Jews into believing Jesus had been resurrected and was therefore their Messiah. Aside from this being far-fetched from a scientific standpoint, it offends everything that is known about

> "Our faith rests on the historicity of these Gospel facts. Christians believe in facts. Some religions have their foundations in myth, fraud, or philosophy, but Christianity rests on something that actually happened."

His character and teaching. How could such a nefarious fraud be reconciled with the ethics He taught? Would One whose life and ministry is celebrated for its kindness, goodness and honesty be part of such deception? Would the apostles stake their lives on claims they knew to be false?

In view of such claims, therefore, a study of Christ's resurrection begins with the actuality of His death. The biblical details of events leading to the cross, the cruel murder itself, as well as what was done with the body afterward leave no possibility of His having survived. Jesus was dead and pronounced dead in the late afternoon of Friday, Nissan 14 (Jewish calendar), before a crowd of witnesses.

> *Why would nonbelievers feel they need to give a rational explanation of the resurrection story?*
>
> . . . .
>
> *What are two theories that seek to explain how Jesus might have been still alive when buried?*

No Mistaken Identity

Who was the person crucified? Some Muslims hold that the man who died on the cross was not Jesus. Others, limited only by their own irreverent imagination, suppose a scheme in which an imposter was crucified in His place, making it possible for the real Jesus later to present Himself as having been resurrected. Unfortunately, many prefer to accept fiction rather than bothering with investigation. To assume, however, that the soldiers, for whatever reason, crucified the wrong person cannot be reconciled with the biblical record, and there is no other record! After over three years of public ministry no one was better known than Jesus. He had entered Jerusalem that week with multitudes praising Him as "the Prophet Jesus, from Nazareth in Galilee." During the week, He taught openly in the temple, and the blind and many came to Him for healing. Even His enemies had seen His miracles and had been so often rebuffed in face-to-face confrontations as to know His features well. None doubted that it was Jesus who drove the merchants and money changers from the temple. The Sanhedrin's failure to arrest Him in public was not because they could not identify Him, but because among the people, He was too well-known and admired. Their arrangement with Judas, His betrayer, would be to locate Him in darkness in a secluded place.

After the last supper, He had gone with His disciples to Gethsemane, a garden on the Mount of Olives. He asked them to wait while He prayed. With only Peter, James, and John close, a solitary place was found for prayer. Never has there been a prayer comparable to the words He raised to heaven in that dark night. Yet even such words of distress and dread fail to convey the pathos that wracked His soul and body. Afterward, though, being strengthened by an angel, He awakened the disciples and went to face the mob He knew was coming.

Included in the arresting party were scribes, elders, chief priests, servants, and both Jewish and Roman soldiers. They came armed as if seeking a dangerous robber. In the dancing shadows cast by torches and lanterns, faces might not be recognized, but Jesus immediately identified Himself.

> "Whom are you seeking?" They answered Him, "Jesus of Nazareth." Jesus said to them, "I am He." And Judas, who betrayed Him, also stood with them. Now when He said to them, "I am He," they drew back and fell to the ground. Then He asked them again, "Whom are you seeking?" And they said, "Jesus of Nazareth." Jesus answered, "I have told you that I am He" (John 18:4-8a).

In the immediate confusion, Judas quickly acted on his treacherous bargain with the Pharisees. Being one of the 12 and certainly able to distinguish between Jesus and the others, he had struck a deal with the priests to lead them to Jesus. "Whomever I kiss, He is the One; seize Him." Better it would have been had this betrayer had never been born (Matthew 26:48), but the point is that Judas's kiss helped insure it was Jesus they were arresting.

From the moment He was taken into custody until He was taken down from the cross, there was not a moment when He was not under the watch of large numbers. Not once was He allowed to be alone or to be with His disciples and friends. No plot to exchange victims was possible. At hearings before the Jews and in the Roman courts, none questioned that the man before them was Jesus of Nazareth. Crowds saw Him at His trials and crowds watched Him taken to Golgotha, including His closest friends. These were women and men who had followed Him from Galilee.

> *From the last supper with the Twelve until His last breath, was there any possibility that it was not Jesus who was arrested, tried, and crucified?*

Exhausting Hours (Matthew 26:36-27:26; Mark 14:26-15:15; Luke22:39-23:25; John 18:1-19:16)

By ordinary human standards, Jesus was already physically and emotionally exhausted long before the crucifixion nails were driven. The last supper on Thursday evening was followed by hard conversations before leaving the city. The walk to Gethsemane was down through the Kidron ravine and up the slope of the Mount of Olives.

The disciples, exhausted by sadness and uncertainty, could not stay awake. But Jesus, without rest, spent an hour in agonizing prayer. First kneeling, then falling prostrate, He prayed with such intensity that "His sweat became like great drops of blood falling down to the ground" (Luke 22:24). He described Himself as being "exceedingly sorrowful, even unto death" (Matthew 26:38, Mark 14:34). The passion that would climax in His death was already tearing at His soul. Soon the soldiers and clerics arrived, and then for every hour until He died, He was subjected to cruel abuse.

He was bound either by ropes or manacles and was marched back up the city. He was taken first to the house of Annas, where during questioning, He was struck by one of the officers. Kept bound, they moved Him from there to the court of Caiaphas. It was Caiaphas who only weeks before had declared to the council that, for the sake of the nation, Jesus had to die. This had set into motion official plans to kill Him (John 11:46-53). At this pretense of a hearing, Jesus silently endured accusations, blasphemy, and mockery. They slapped Him and spit in His face. They blindfolded and beat Him with their fists. Such was endured through the rest of the night, until at early dawn, He was brought into the council's chamber, where under the pretense of official action, they hatefully and hastily pronounced a sentence of death.

Being under Roman occupation, they could not themselves carry out executions. They bound Him again and took Him to the Roman governor, where they met Pilate outside his palace, so as not to be defiled before the Passover. Pilate's first response was to pass responsibility back to the Jews, but their protests pressured him to take Jesus inside for an interview. Nothing he heard justified capital punishment. He went back to the Jews and declared, "I find no fault in Him at all" (John 18:38). But their accusations were not in the least softened.

Having learned Jesus was from Galilee and apparently wanting neither to offend the Jews nor to kill an innocent man, Pilate thought to pass responsibility to Herod, whose jurisdiction was Galilee, but who happened to be in Jerusalem at the time. There was no reason for Jesus to explain anything to Herod. So, after hearing the vehement accusation of the priests and scribes, Herod and his soldiers spent some time mocking the Man and sent Him back to Pilate.

With Jesus back in his court and knowing that neither he nor Herod had found Him guilty, he proposed a solution that he hoped would close the matter. It was his custom to release a prisoner during the time of Passover. This time he would offer the Jews a choice. Which of two men would they want released: Jesus or a prisoner named Barabbas, a notorious insurrectionist and murderer? Surely, Pilate thought, they would make the reasonable choice and allow Jesus to be set free, but he under estimated the rage of the Jews. They wanted Barabbas. "What then shall I do with Jesus who is called Christ?" They became even more vehement, "Let Him be crucified." But Pilate kept insisting, "Why, what evil has He done?"

> "Hoping that the hateful demands of the Jews would now be satisfied, Pilate had Jesus brought back before the mob. He was clothed in a purple robe and wearing a thorn-barbed crown."

Unable to assuage the mob, Pilate next thought he might appease them by simply having Jesus punished. The punishment would be scourging, a barbaric torture in which the prisoner was tied to a post and flogged mercilessly. The Bible does not describe the savagery involved, but typically in Roman practice these floggings were executed with whips embedded with pieces of metal or bone designed to rip into naked flesh. Victims were tied to a post, sometimes in a bent position. The whip could rip away pieces of flesh. Sometimes, depending on the barbarity of the soldier, it would be applied to the face and belly. We are left to our own mental image of our Lord's physical condition after inhuman torture.

Hoping that the hateful demands of the Jews would now be satisfied, Pilate had Jesus brought back before the mob. He was clothed in a purple robe and wearing a thorn-barbed crown. Partly out of sarcasm and partly hoping the Jews might have some pity when they saw His condition, Pilate announced, "Behold the Man!" It was as if he was saying, "Look at His pitiable condition. He is no threat to you. Let me release Him." It was not enough. They demanded crucifixion. Mocking them, Pilate said, "You take Him and crucify Him, for I find no fault in Him." They would not relent. "We have a law, and according to our law He ought to die, because He made Himself the Son of God" (John 19:4-7).

Back inside the Praetorium and after further questioning, the governor again was determined that Jesus ought to be released, but the Jews threatened, "If you let this Man go, you are not Caesar's friend. Whoever makes himself a king speaks against Caesar" (John 19:12). They were willing to charge Pilate himself with treason. Pilate, now threatened with blackmail, took his place at the seat of judgment and had Jesus brought before them again. Yielded to the pressure of the mob, Jesus was turned over to the soldiers for death by crucifixion.

Having received such orders, nothing was left to constrain the godless and cruel soldiers. The entire garrison gathered to resume the mocking and beating. They had a victim to kill, so let them make the most of it. He had been scourged earlier when Pilate had thought such would placate His accusers, but more torture was typical Roman practice for men sentenced to die. If more flogging was involved, it could be as brutal as brutal men could make it. Their only restraint was that He still be alive when they got to Golgotha. The sentence required execution on a cross, but taking Him "half-dead" to Golgotha would speed the process.

> *Why would nonbelievers feel they need to give a rational explanation of the resurrection story?*
>
> . . . .
>
> *What are two theories that seek to explain how Jesus might have been still alive when buried?*

Crucified (Matthew 27:31-37; Mark 15:20-48; Luke 23:26-46; John 18:17-19:30)

It is usually explained that Simon of Cyrene was conscripted to carry the cross because Jesus was now too weak to bear it. He had Himself been led away carrying it before Simon took over. Actually, the Bible does not give an explanation as to why Simon became involved. It does not say Jesus fell under the weight. When, however, we consider the long hours, the distances He had walked while bound, having had no food, drink or rest, and the way He was abused, beaten and scourged: utter exhaustion is a reasonable explanation.

It was about 9:00 on Friday morning, the day before the Passover Sabbath, when they brought Him outside the city gate to "the Place of the Skull" (Hebrew, Golgotha; Latin, Calvary).

Two men, criminals, were brought to be executed beside Him. A notice would be posted — "Jesus of Nazareth, King of the Jews." He was offered a drink of sour wine mixed with a bitter herb. This was intended as an analgesic, but He refused to drink. He was stripped of His clothing and nailed to the cross.

The Roman method of crucifixion involved the victim laid on his back on a wooden beam with arms outstretched. Spikes were driven through the hands (or wrists). The cross beam was fastened to a post into which would be nailed the victim's feet. The cross was then raised up with the foot of the timber being pushed into a hole. The Gospel writers do not indulge in lurid details, but it is obvious that suffering was greatly intensified by the body's weight pulling against the wounds. Much of the agony was the unrelieved sense of asphyxiation as the victim struggled to inhale. Only by pulling and pushing against the wounds could lungs be expanded to inhale. For six hours, Jesus' breast heaved for air until He took His last breath. In mid-afternoon Jesus was dead.

The Gospel writers give overlapping descriptions of the moment of Jesus' death. He "cried out with a loud voice, and breathed His last" (Mark 15:37). "He said, "Father, 'into Your hands I commit My spirit.' Having said this, He breathed His last" (Luke 23:46). "And Jesus cried out again with a loud voice, and yielded up His spirit" (Matthew 27:50). "He said, 'It is finished!' And bowing His head, He gave up His spirit" (John 19:30). He chose His own moment to die. Though by the hands of others, the death of Christ was voluntary, all in the will of His Father.

> Therefore My Father loves Me, because I lay down My
> life that I may take it again. No one takes it from Me,

> but I lay it down of Myself. I have power
> to lay it down, and I have power to take it again.
> This command I have received from My Father
> (John 10:17-18).

How brutal would the soldiers be expected to be when preparing a victim for crucifixion?

. . . .

What are some aspects of crucifixion that especially contributed to the victim's agony?

This does not exonerate the Jews and Romans involved, but all was in the Divine purpose. Various plots and attacks had been made against His life, but none succeeded. Because of the love of the Father, however, our Savior willingly became the sacrifice for our sins. And it was because of that same love that He would arise.

Death Witnessed (Matthew 27:51-56; Mark 15:39-41; Luke 23:47-49; John 19:31-37)

Sometimes a victim's legs were broken to make him less able to raise himself, escalating suffocation and hastening death. At the request of the Jewish leaders, who wanted the bodies removed before the Sabbath, Pilate ordered the victims' legs to be broken. Probably a wooden club or mallet would be used to crush the bones. The shattered limbs would no longer be able to push against the metal rods in their feet as the victims struggled to inhale. But after finishing the merciless task on the other two, they found Jesus already dead. His legs were not broken. The centurion, the officer in charge of the Roman death squad, was directly in front watching carefully. He would not have vacated the governor's order had he not been certain Jesus was dead. He had never seen anyone die in the way Jesus died. An innocent Man had chosen His own moment to give up His life and declared it with the voice of One who while dying was still in control.

Then one of the soldiers, either out of grisly contempt or merely intending to make death certain, shoved a spear into Jesus' side. As the opened wound would be as large as a man's hand, the blade must have been wide before tapering to its point. Likely the blow was with an upward thrust, tearing through muscle, lungs, and heart. Blood and water ran out of the wound. Life is in the blood, and bloodshed means death. Scientific opinions vary as to the medical significance of both water and blood issuing together. Regardless, this soldier's gruesome act proved death was certain. It was a ghastly spectacle, indisputable evidence that death was complete.

The apostle John watched it happen, and in his Gospel, he makes pointed reference to having been present. Later when John wrote about what he had seen, he realized all had been foretold in the prophecy. He thought of Psalm 34:20, when he wrote, "Not one of His bones shall be broken," and another that said, "They shall look on Him whom they pierced," (a reference to Zechariah 12:10). John was certain about what he had seen. "And he who has seen has testified, and his testimony is true; and he knows that he is telling the truth, so that you may believe" (John 19:35-36).

A great multitude of men and women had followed to the cross and also watched Jesus die. The centurion would certify to the governor what he had seen (Mark 15:44-45). The chief priests and scribes were there. They knew life Jesus was dead. Later, when they asked Pilate to secure the grave, they had

*In considering
the history of the
resurrection, why is
it important to know
details related to
Christ's death?*

. . . .

*What details make
it unreasonable to
think Jesus survived
crucifixion?*

. . . .

*What assured John of
Divine involvement in
what he witnessed?*

. . . .

*What about the
centurion shows
he knew death
had occurred?*

. . . .

*Who are other
witnesses, friends and
foes, who could have
attested to His death?*

no doubt that only His lifeless corpse would be within. It may seem superfluous to say it, but at the point a person is dead, he is completely dead. Jesus' body was dead, as dead as any person who ever died!

Every biblical detail pertaining to the last six hours of Jesus' life is worthy of meditation — the jeers of the crowd, His seven words, fulfilled prophecy, its purpose for our redemption, etc. In the story of the resurrection, however, our emphasis is first on the actuality of His death.

CHAPTER TWO

And That He Was Buried

WHEN COMPARED WITH THE PASSION AND PURPOSE OF Christ's death and the glorious power of His resurrection, the burial itself might seem incidental. In summarizing Gospel facts, however, Paul specifically included reference to the burial (1 Corinthians 15:4). The fact is that His grave, its location, the care taken with His corpse, and the tomb having been under military guard are all factors that contribute to the evidence of the resurrection. Considering the brevity of the written records, it is amazing that so much detail is known about the Lord's burial. From the beginning, the debate between Christians and unbelievers has not been over whether His grave was found empty, but over what became of His body.

In some cases, the Romans may have left bodies of crucifixion victims to rot or to be consumed by animals. Such spectacles would be reminders of the harshness of Roman justice. In Jesus' case, the matter was not left to the Romans. They put men on crosses, but it was not their assignment to take them down. As to Jewish regulations, the law of Moses specified that a condemned man who was hanged was not to be left overnight, but was to be taken down and buried (Deuteronomy 21:23). It would be expected that one dying in such an ignominious way would be buried in an appropriately dishonorable way. Both the Deuteronomy requirement and His death having occurred on the eve of Sabbath should have made the Jewish hierarchy not only determined that Jesus was really dead, but also buried the same day. It appears, however, that though they had feverishly pressed for the Romans to carry out the execution, they had not thought ahead about the disposition of the body.

> *What did Jewish law require regarding a felon's body?*
>
> . . . .
>
> *Does it seem the Jewish authorities had thought ahead about its disposal?*

Procuring the Corpse (Matthew 27:57-58; Mark 15:42-45; Luke 23:50-52; John 19:31-38)

It would be expected that families and loyal friends would want to provide a decent burial, but the task would not be easy. First, because it was supposed to be a criminal execution, there would need to be authorization from the governor. Those involved would likely be scorned for their willingness to be identified with a condemned man. Just getting the body down would probably require two or more strong men. Then there was the matter of customary preparation of the corpse, finding a burial place, and providing transportation.

Joseph of Arimathea has not been mentioned previously in the Gospel narrative. The location of his hometown is unknown today, but obviously, he was much involved with the city of Jerusalem and had arranged for his own burial in a garden outside the gate. He was a rich man who was of high rank in the Jewish council, but he had not been a part of the conspiracy against Jesus. He is described as a "good and just man" (Luke 23:50), who had been himself a secret follower of Jesus. He had believed the promise of the coming kingdom and kept that hope even after Jesus died. John is the only one of the 12 actually named as having stood close to the cross to the end. Joseph, however, must have been among the nearby spectators and seeing it was over, mustered courage to approach Pilate to request the body. As a prominent member of the Sanhedrin, he was given immediate audience with the governor.

Throughout that busy Friday, members of the hate-filled Jewish hierarchy had gone to Pilate to pressure him to murder an innocent man. A short time later they rushed back to Pilate to protest the sign that had indicted Jesus as "King of the Jews." A third time they came to ask for the victims' bones to be broken. Now, another Jew, Joseph, himself also a ruler of the people, came with a completely different purpose. He wanted authority to remove and care for the body. We might imagine confusion on Pilate's part over such divergent purposes.

> "Crucifixion was designed to cause lingering agony... The difference in Jesus' case is that He chose for Himself when to die."

The governor was surprised to hear that Jesus was already dead. Crucifixion was designed to cause lingering agony. It was not supposed to be a quick death. The difference in Jesus' case is that He chose for Himself when to die (John 10:18). Before granting permission, therefore, Pilate sent for the centurion, the officer who had overseen the entire horrific proceedings. This soldier would not be mistaken. He knew when a man was dead. It is unlikely that he shared with Pilate his own impressions of the divine dignity with which the Savior had passed. He did, however, certify for the governor that indeed the prisoner was dead. Permission was granted for Joseph to take the body. It was Preparation Day (our Friday) in the evening before beginning of the Sabbath.

> *What were the several reasons the Jews had gone to Pilate?*
>
> . . . .
>
> *Why would Joseph have had ready access to the governor?*

The Undertakers

The lifeless form had to be lifted off the nails and carried to the tomb. Though this was nearby, Joseph would need help. There is no indication that any of the 11 apostles or any of Jesus' family were involved. John had been present to watch Jesus die, but may have left the scene to care for Mary at his home. It is possible that a man of Joseph's position would have servants, but Nicodemus is the only helper named. He is identified as also having been a ruler of the Jews and is the same Nicodemus who had a nighttime interview with Jesus in the first year of the Lord's ministry (John 3). Three times the Bible identifies him as the Nicodemus who had come to Jesus at night. There had been one occasion when he argued in the Council that Jesus should not be condemned without a fair hearing.

But when his protest was ridiculed, it seems he ceased to argue (John 7:50-51). Now these two formerly secret disciples would openly take charge of the burial.

It is not known how soon Nicodemus arrived, but it's likely he was also in the crowd with Joseph, and when he saw Jesus die, he had hurried to get burial spices and return. Joseph had purchased clean linen cloth. How and where it was bought is not told. Nicodemus brought 100 pounds of spices, a mixture of myrrh and aloes. It is interesting that Joseph provided only the cloth and Nicodemus only the spices, though each would have known both items were needed. This suggests that they had previously arranged what each would do.

The large quantity of spices would have been quite expensive and was indicative of great love and respect for the Master. Only a few days before, Mary, the sister of Martha and Lazarus, had anointed Jesus' head and feet with a costly ointment. It was spikenard, an oil used for soothing and perfuming the skin. Its great cost caused the disciples, especially Judas, to criticize her for not making a more practical use of something so valuable. The Lord, however, received it as something of greater significance. "She has come beforehand to anoint My body for burial" (Mark 14:3; Matthew 26:6; John 12:2). Alive or dead Jesus would be honored. For Mary, Joseph, and Nicodemus, expense was not an issue. It is always in order to be extravagant for Christ!

What suggests that Joseph and Nicodemus had previously planned for Jesus' burial?

. . . .

Did Mary and the disciples understand the real significance of the costly ointment?

Preparing the Body (Matthew 27:59-60; Mark 14:46; Luke 23:53-54; John 19:39-42)

Jewish burial custom involved washing the corpse. There is no specific reference to this, but it seems reasonable that some cleansing would have been done. "Then they took the body of Jesus, and bound it in strips of linen with the spices, as the custom of the Jews is to bury" (John 19:40). Instead of a single sheet, they wrapped swaths of cloth around the body and limbs and layered spices within the folds of the bandages. This was the best they knew about retarding decomposition and preserving a corpse. They may have also spread a layer of spices on the burial slab. A separate piece of cloth was used to cover His face. It is important to understand that more was involved than just a covering draped over the body. We can understand the extent of such binding by comparing the account of the raising of Lazarus. When Jesus had called him out of the tomb he was "bound hand and foot with graveclothes, and his face was wrapped with a cloth." It was necessary for the bandages to be removed to let him go (John 11:44).

It was an arduous and tearful process. Exposed to them were the ghastly wounds caused by the nails, the gruesome tear made by the soldier's spear, and the ripped gashes inflicted earlier by the scourging whip. All would be done hastily because Sabbath was soon to begin. The corpse was laid on the slab and a cloth was laid over His head. The heavy stone door was rolled into place, and the grave was closed.

In the late Medieval Ages, claims began to be made of the discovery of a sheet, which was the actual cloth that had been wrapped around Jesus' body: the Shroud of Turin. It supposedly shows stains that would be consistent with wounds caused by crucifixion. Of course, even if they indicate evidence of crucifixion, there is no way to ascertain who was the victim. However, in some circles, there has been much excitement about this supposed "sacred" cloth, but the claims do not match the details of Scripture. In the first place, instead of a single covering from head to feet, a separate cloth covered the face. Further, the Bible speaks of cloths (plural). No mention is made of a single covering for the whole body (John 20:6-7). The Shroud, like other supposed relics associated with Christ, may be intriguing to some, but our faith is in the inspired history of Holy Scripture.

Was His body wrapped in a single sheet?

. . . .

How does the case of Lazarus help us understand the thoroughness of the wrapping?

. . . .

What was the purpose they had for this process?

The Sepulcher

The crucifixion had been at the place called Golgotha. Though traditions locate it, the actual spot is uncertain. Neither do we know anything specific about the surroundings, except that it was outside the city gate and not far from a garden. References to gardens usually suggest quiet places with trees and other vegetation. In this garden was a burial chamber that Joseph had recently prepared for himself. John specifically informs us that no one had yet been buried there. If there had been, the decay of that body might have left an odor of decomposition. No smell of death could come from the grave of Him who could suffer no corruption (Acts 13:36-37). This also counters any claims the Jews might have made about how the body might have revived. In Old Testament history, a man was hastily laid in Elisha's grave. When the bones of the prophet were touched, the man revived (2 Kings 13:21). But no claim could be made that Jesus came to life by contact with the bones of another. Such would admittedly have been a miracle itself, but the Lord's enemies might argue it as less significant than that Jesus had arisen by His own divine power.

The sepulcher was carved into rock and consisted of a room that could be entered by stooping down. It was cut into a hillside as a cave. Typically, shelves would be cut into the wall for the placement of family members when the need arose. Such a tomb would only be afforded for someone of wealth. That Jesus, poor by earthly standards, would be buried in such a place was foreseen in prophecy. "And they made His grave with the wicked — But with the rich at His death" (Isaiah 53:9).

A tourist site in modern Jerusalem known as "The Church of the Holy Sepulcher" is supposed to have been erected over the actual tomb. In the immediate vicinity, there are other rock-hewn tombs from the same time period. There is also archaeological evidence of a burial slab under the structure, but it is impossible to know who, if anyone, was ever buried there. Claims have been made for other sites in the same area, and tombs have been found, which resemble what we know from the Bible record. The value of archaeology is that it establishes that such tombs existed in the same area and in the same time period. Whether, in fact, we could know the spot where our Lord once lay, we can be certain such a tomb existed, and that at the time, its location was well-known to friend and foe alike. Whatever the exact location doesn't matter. It was only used for part of three days.

In contrast, the tombs of the founders of other religions are well-known to their followers. Confucius (Buddhism) is in a grave in China. Mary Baker Eddy (The Church of Christ, Scientist) is buried in Cambridge, Massachusetts. Joseph Smith

(Mormonism) in Nauvoo, Illinois. Muhammed's (Islam) body is in Medina. Islam makes no claim for an empty tomb. Their "prophet," and all other such pretenders, are still dead.

It is useful in this connection to remember how Jesus had foretold His death, burial, and resurrection as having been portrayed in the case of Jonah. "For as Jonah was three days and three nights in the belly of the great fish, so will the Son of Man be three days and three nights in the heart of the earth" (Matthew 12:40). "Heart of" meant the interior, inside the ground, as opposed to being above ground. Such would be complete enclosure, whether in the dirt or in a mausoleum. Paul appropriated this fact in reference to the conversion process. We are "buried with Him in baptism" (Colossians 2:12; Romans 6:3-4). The purpose of burial is to put the remains out of sight (Genesis 23:4). The immersion of baptism is a covering out of sight, so to speak, of the lost man in re-enactment of Jesus being put out of sight in the ground.

They laid Jesus to rest and rolled the stone over the door. His corpse was left alone inside the vault. When the door was opened, there could be only one body inside — rather in this case, no body at all!

What are two reasons it might have been important to know the tomb had not been previously used?

. . . .

To what extent have archaeological discoveries proven the Bible to be correct?

. . . .

How did Jesus compare His burial place to the belly of Jonah's fish?

. . . .

What is meant by "in the heart of"?

Women Watched (Matthew 27:61; Mark 15:47; Luke 23:55-56)

The women who had come with Jesus to Jerusalem from Galilee were in the crowds who watched His execution. This included many loyal women, several of whom followed to watch the burial. The specific mention of Mary Magdalene and Mary the mother of Joses does not mean others were not present. They are named because they along with Salome and other women would be the first to find the grave open on Sunday morning. They had stayed to watch as the body was laid inside and the heavy door had been rolled into place. Then, fully satisfied that all had been done and knowing exactly where Jesus was securely interred, "they returned and prepared spices and fragrant oils. And they rested on the Sabbath according to the commandment" (Luke 23:56).

These spices, as was the 100-pound mixture of myrrh and aloes provided by Nicodemus, were intended to delay inevitable decay and odor. However, they could not go back to the crypt until after the Sabbath was past. Regardless of the Jewish leaders' disregard for the law in so many other things, the authorities were strict about observance of Sabbath rules. Ordinarily, some license might have been allowed when attending to the dead, but in this case, the dead was a condemned criminal, undeserving of care. These godly women would keep the Sabbath and prudently avoid calling unnecessary attention to being followers of the Nazarene. So, for two restless nights and through a long day of helplessness, they grieved and waited until they could resume their mission.

The point to be emphasized is that the location of the grave was common knowledge. There was no expectation for privacy and no possibility for secrecy. The location would be known by any who cared or were curious. The spectacle at Calvary had been seen by too many people for the extraordinary disposal of

Is it reasonable to think Christ's women followers would not have known the tomb's location?

. . . .

What are some factors that indicate there would have been official and general knowledge about the tomb?

the body to be ignored. It was a curious thing that a condemned man was being buried in a rich man's tomb and that two prominent and respected members of the Sanhedrin were in charge. Certainly, the chief priests and Pharisees knew where and how of His burial. Some of them, or at least their spies, would watch the proceeding from beginning to end. There was never any doubt on their part as to location and circumstances.

His Sabbath Rest

Once during a busy time in His ministry, Jesus said, "I must work the works of Him that sent Me while it is day; the night is coming when no one can work" (John 9:4). Some translations vary between the singular ("I") and plural ("we"). Either way the word affirms the same reality. Activities cease at death. Jesus was pointing to His coming night when His earthly work would be complete. At the cross, His work was finished (John 19:30). Yes, His spirit went into the spirit world, but His flesh lay lifeless. "For there is no work or device or knowledge or wisdom in the grave..." (Ecclesiastes 9:10). Jesus' lifeless body would remain at rest from late Friday afternoon until early Sunday morning. The day in between was the Sabbath.

God rested on the seventh day after He had completed creation and saw that all was good. The point about God's resting is that His creation work was finished. Centuries later, He would give the Sabbath law to Israel to provide them a day of rest as a reminder that they had not rested under the taskmasters in Egypt (Deuteronomy 5:15). Though Christ's death would bring about the end of the Jewish system and bring in a new covenant, which would not include the Sabbath law, on this Sabbath, the body of Jesus would rest in the grave.

Death is separation of the spirit from the body (James 2:26). In dying, Jesus surrendered His spirit to the Father (Luke 23:46). We know from the promise to the penitent thief that He entered into Paradise (Luke 23:43). There is nothing in the Scriptures about any activity or experience by His spirit while separated from His body and in Paradise.

A misunderstanding of 1 Peter 3:18-20 has caused some to think that while His body was dead, His spirit was on a preaching mission to souls in torment.

> For Christ also suffered once for sins, the just for the unjust, that He might bring us to God, being put to death in the flesh but made alive by the Spirit, by whom also He went and preached to the spirits in prison, who formerly were disobedient, when once the Divine longsuffering waited in the days of Noah, while the ark was being prepared, in which a few, that is, eight souls, were saved through water.

Peter's purpose was to encourage suffering Christians by reminding them that though Christ's body had died, His spirit remained alive. As noted from James 2:26, it is a fact that the body without the spirit is dead, but the opposite is not true. The spirit without the body is alive. In fact, Christ's spirit was

Where was Jesus while His body was in the grave?

. . . .

How was the Sabbath related to creation and to Israel's having been in Egypt?

. . . .

How does Peter's statement assure the difference between body and spirit?

. . . .

Though not so stated in the Scriptures, how might Jesus' time in the tomb be considered His Sabbath rest?

always alive, and as one evidence of that, Peter says that it was by His spirit that He had preached to the antediluvians. They were in "prison" at the time Peter wrote, but the time when Christ had preached to them was during the time of their disobedience, which was while the ark was being built. In the absence of any other explanation in Scripture, we may assume this refers to His Spirit working through Noah, who was "a preacher of righteousness" (2 Peter 2:5). In the above text, therefore, there is no allusion to Christ preaching anywhere to anyone during the time His spirit was separated from His body. When Christ's spirit left His body, He went into Paradise, not into the prison of the condemned.

CHAPTER THREE

The Third Day

THAT JESUS SHOULD BE KILLED BECAME OFFICIAL JEWISH policy under the influence and advice of Caiaphas, the high priest. As reports came about the raising of Lazarus at nearby Bethany, the council met to deliberate how best to deal with Jesus' growing influence and favor with the people. The council's self-justification was national political expediency. They were under the rule of Rome and if Jesus' following continued to grow, they argued, it could upset the delicate balance of their relationship with Rome. "If we let Him alone like this, everyone will believe in Him, and the Romans will come and take away both our place and nation. Then, from that day on, they plotted to put Him to death" (John 11:45-53).

But when He was brought to trial, even Pilate would recognize their motivation was really envy. Their one objective before Pilate was that Jesus be crucified and that it should be done as soon as possible. For six hours they had watched their murderous purpose performed. Death could be hastened by breaking the victims' legs. Bone-crushing blows shattered the legs of the two criminals, but when the soldiers came to Jesus, they found Him already dead. The centurion did not hesitate to cancel Pilate's order. He had seen how Jesus breathed His last. So remarkable was the manner of his death that he said, "Truly this man was the Son of God" (Mark 15:39).

In their fervor to have Jesus killed, it seems the Jewish rulers had given no immediate thought to the disposal of the body. Now that it was done and realizing the next day was the High Sabbath of Passover, they realized that it would be politically inappropriate to leave the bodies hanging. Of yet more concern was the possibility that even dead, Jesus could still have influence with the people. They knew that Jesus had promised, "After three days I will rise again" (Matthew 27:63). It would be absurd that they could admit such possibility and yet refuse to accept His Messiahship. Nevertheless, whether they believed He could actually arise, there was no denying that He had done many mighty works, including having raised others, such as Lazarus.

> "A large heavy stone, which was shaped to fit the entrance, had been rolled into place. Once in place, it could not easily be removed."

Jesus' promise would especially concern the Pharisees. Unlike the Sadducees, their theology accepted the possibility of resurrection. They could hardly say to the public no such thing was possible. They knew the people had seen His power. Things were already getting beyond their control. Any unusual event would stir public imagination.

If the grave were found empty, if the body went missing, they might lose what was left of their influence over the people. They had hated the Man Jesus alive. Now they feared losing control over the Man Jesus dead.

The fast action by Joseph and Nicodemus likely caught them by surprise. We can imagine their frustration and scorn when they realized that prominent members of their own high council were actually the Nazarene's friends. Matthew tells us that it was "the next day which followed the Day of Preparation" (Matthew 27:62) when they went again to Pilate to ask that the tomb be secured with a guard. The Preparation Day was Friday. The next day was the Sabbath, but by Jewish time that next day actually began at sunset on Friday. Haste was needed because if the disciples were going to steal the body, it could be in the darkness of that same night. During the early hours of Friday, their false piety had kept them from being defiled by entering Pilate's chambers. Now, after the crowds were gone, a few of the chief priests and Pharisees went to meet with the governor privately. By meeting with the governor in the early hours of the Sabbath, they violated their own Sabbath scruples. Sin always compounds itself. We can image Pilate's contempt for their obvious hypocrisy and continued demands.

> "Sir, we remember, while He was still alive, how that deceiver said, 'After three days I will rise.' Therefore command that the tomb be made secure until the third day, lest His disciples come by night and steal Him away, and say to the people, 'He has risen from the dead.' So the last deception will be worse than the first" (Matthew 27:63-64).

They never referred to Jesus by His name, only as "that deceiver." In no way could they allow Pilate to think they were concerned about more than political expediency. That they only requested the guard until "the third day" underscores how seriously they had considered Jesus' words. The request to Pilate appealed to his desire to avoid civil unrest. There was, of course, no evidence that the disciples intended to steal the body. A conspiracy to make people believe Jesus was alive would make no sense nor offer any advantage. The disciples' expectations and endeavors ended when Jesus was nailed to the tree. It is a marvel that these Pharisees so assiduously remembered what the disciples appeared to forget. Again, we wonder what His enemies really feared. There is a wonderful irony in their being so determined to prevent the body from disappearing. As it would happen, the empty grave would be one of the "many infallible proofs" that Jesus was alive.

"Pilate said to them, 'You have a guard; go your way, make it as secure as you know how.' So they went and made the tomb secure, sealing the stone and setting the guard" (Matthew 27:65-66). Roman soldiers, not temple officers, would provide maximum security. The Jewish leaders did not simply send the soldiers. They went with them and affixed the seal themselves. The tomb had been carefully carved into solid rock. A large heavy stone, which was shaped to fit the entrance, had been rolled into place. Once in place, it could not easily be removed. No details are given as to how the seal was affixed, but it signified by the authority of Rome that the door was not to be opened. That authority was to be enforced by an armed squad: "Make it as secure as you know how." The Jews would have monitored everything carefully. Any disturbance would have to be beyond human control.

How many guards? The whole garrison had been involved in the mocking of Jesus before He was led to Golgotha. Roman soldiers had been involved in His arrest. At least four soldiers and a centurion were involved in the crucifixion, possibly more. One had stabbed the corpse with a spear. Whether it was the same men or others who were given this duty, they had to be aware of the extraordinary events of that weekend and of the unrest that engulfed the city. It was a strange mission, safeguarding the closed grave of a man that they (or at least their comrades) had mocked, beaten, and crucified. They had stolen His clothing and gambled over it, but now were making sure His corpse was not disturbed.

What must have been their thoughts and conversation as they stood their posts in the garden? But as soldiers, it was not their place to question orders. At other times and in other places, other tombs had been guarded, even by soldiers, but never to prevent the person they murdered from being raised from the dead!

How might they have known that Jesus had specified the third day to His disciples?

. . . .

Why were the Jews so concerned with Jesus' "third day" predictions?

. . . .

Did any of His enemies believe a resurrection was possible?

. . . .

What did they say to justify their request to Pilate?

. . . .

What is the significance of a Roman seal and Roman guards?

First Lord's Day (Matthew 28:1-4; Mark 16:1-2; Luke 24:1; John 20:1)

All four Gospel narratives identify the day as the "first day of the week" — our Sunday. Jesus was killed on the day of the Passover sacrifice, Nissan 14 on the Jews' calendar, which that year occurred on a Friday. He was buried the same day and was in the grave throughout the next day, the Jewish Sabbath, our Saturday. In recognition that it was on Sunday that He arose, Christians properly call Sunday "the Lord's Day" (Revelation 1:10).

Special days are commemorated because of special events. Because it is His resurrection that gives validity to all we believe, from the church's beginning His death is remembered in the Lord's Supper every Lord's Day. "This is the day the Lord has made; We will rejoice and be glad in it" (Psalm 118:24).

Some have unnecessary concern over Jesus' saying His time in the tomb would be "three days and three nights" (Matthew 12:40). If it is supposed that this meant three 24-hour periods (i.e., 72 hours), which would require a longer time than from Friday afternoon to Sunday morning. However, this wording must be compared to the other ways He and the apostles expressed the time.

- In Mark 8:31 and John 2:19, Jesus said it would be "in three days."
- At other times, He said it would be on the "third day" (Matthew 16:21; et al).
- Peter and Paul also said it was on the "third day" (Acts 10:40; 1 Corinthians 15:4).
- His enemies also understood His meaning and wanted the grave guarded "until the third day" (Matthew 27:64).

If by "three days and three nights" a full 72 hours had been intended, the resurrection would have been on the fourth day instead of the third. Rather than pressing unnecessary literalness, therefore, it is better to recognize the common practice (then and now) of counting part of a day as a day. "Three days and three nights" was a way of referring to three calendar days without identifying how much of each day was intended. When Jesus promised it would be on the "third day," He meant the third after the crucifixion. As He was crucified on Friday, the third day was Sunday.

We are not told the exact time the body of Jesus came back to life. The earthquake had occurred sometime before sun-up. As an earthquake coincided with the moment of His death, so it may be that this one coincided with the moment He arose. It was still dark when Mary arrived at the opened tomb and the guards were already gone. All that we can know is that it was in the hours of darkness sometime before sunrise.

Neither is there any description of the event itself. It is sufficient to know it happened. Curiosity and imagination might raise many questions about the resurrection event itself. Did He suddenly open His eyes? Was there a quick movement? Did He push Himself up slowly, or was He instantly upright? Was a sound made? Did His awakening coincide with the earthquake? How quickly were the linen wrappings put aside and what kind of clothing would replace the garments that had been confiscated at the cross? Did the Father call for Him to rise? Was it like when Jesus had called for others to come back to life?

When Jesus raised Jairus's daughter He took her by the hand and said, "Little girl, arise" (Mark 5:41, Luke 8:54). Lazarus had been called out of his grave by Jesus shouting, "Lazarus, come forth" (John 11:43). Ordinary writers would have exhausted imagery to portray so dramatic an event. The attention of

Scripture, however, is not on the resurrection event itself, but on the fact that it happened.

It might be questioned whether Jesus arose on His own or whether His Father raised Him. A determination is unnecessary because it is expressed both ways in many passages (e.g. 1 Corinthians 6:14; John 10:17). The thing to be understood is that it was altogether by divine power. Nothing of human science, psychology, or philosophy was involved. On a certain Sunday, an actual date in history, the Savior's corpse came back to life. No serum was administered, no current was applied, no incantations were performed. "For though He was crucified in weakness, yet He lives by the power of God" (2 Corinthians 13:4). He who is the source of all life put life into the lifeless form. "For to this end Christ died and rose and lived again, that He might be Lord of both the dead and the living" (Romans 14:9).

> *On which day of the week was Jesus crucified?*
>
> . . . .
>
> *Was Jesus raised on the Sabbath?*
>
> . . . .
>
> *How different are the statements as to the time reconciled?*
>
> . . . .
>
> *In what way are the Lord's Supper and the Lord's Day connected?*

First to Arise (Acts 26:23)

In Paul's defense before King Agrippa, he affirmed from the prophets "that Christ would suffer, that He would be the first to rise from the dead." We know that there had been other resurrections (e. g. Lazarus), but Paul says Jesus was first. One difference in Jesus' case is that "Christ, having been raised from the dead, dies no more. Death no longer has dominion over Him" (Romans 6:9). The others eventually died again. Jesus alone can say, "I am He who lives, and was dead, and behold, I am alive forevermore" (Revelation 1:18). In the Hebrews discussion of Him as our High Priest, it is assured, "Therefore He is also able to save to the uttermost those who come to God through Him, since He always lives to make intercession for them" (Hebrews 7:28).

The point also is that His being the first raised implies that others would follow. Christians are promised their own resurrection to life eternal because Christ was raised and forever lives. In making this point, Paul alludes to the Old Testament offering up the firstfruits of harvest (Leviticus 23:10-11).

The first sheaf was raised up before the Lord as representative of the full harvest that would follow. "But now Christ is risen from the dead, and has become the firstfruits of those who have fallen asleep... But each one in his own order: Christ the firstfruits, afterward those who are Christ's at His coming" (1 Corinthians 15:20, 23).

Is it necessary to understand how the resurrection happened before we can believe in it?

How is the resurrection of Jesus different from others who had been raised?

How is the term "firstfruits" connected with the point that Jesus was the first to rise?

The symbolism is more impressive that the firstfruits offering was appointed for the day following the Sabbath, the first day of the week, the day Christ arose. Similarly, He is called "the first-born from the dead" (Colossians 1:18; Revelation 1:5). That is, of all who will be raised, He is the pre-eminent One, the One who leads the way for all others.

Guards' Report (Matthew 28:11-15)

It was still in the shadows of the early dawn before any of the women arrived in the garden.

> And behold, there was a great earthquake; for an angel of the Lord descended from heaven, and came and rolled back the stone from the door, and sat on it. His countenance was like lightning, and his clothing as white as snow. And the guards shook for fear of him, and became like dead men...some of the guard came into the city and reported to the chief priests all the things that had happened (Matthew 28:2-10).

It is not to be assumed that the angel had moved the stone to let Jesus out. His resurrected body was not limited by time or space. (Later, He would suddenly enter a room with the doors being shut.) Instead, the grave was opened to show it was empty. Jesus was already gone. In the purposes of God, Jesus had been held by death long enough. Peter's explanation in Acts 2:24 says, "Whom God raised up, having loosed the pains of death." Death is personified as a snare, a trap, from which there is no escape (Psalm 18:4), but Jesus did escape! Unbreakable chains were broken! He arose! The door is open; the witnesses can come in.

The Roman guards were the first to know that something had happened that was beyond human expectation. Whether when they had regained their senses, they had looked inside, we are not told. We know they did not themselves see Jesus because the record says Mary would be the first. His appearances over the next 40 days would be only to His followers. Some of the soldiers, however, would report the facts of the broken seal and the opened grave. Their report was convincing to those who feared it most.

How much on their own the council investigated the scene, we are not told, but it can be certain they would want verification. If on any basis they could deny the guards' report, they would have denounced the guards to Pilate. The report was true. It was the "third day," and the body of Jesus was no longer where it had been and where, behind a heavy stone, a government seal, and a Roman guard, it had been expected to stay. The body was gone!

> When they had assembled with the elders and consulted together, they gave a large sum of money to the soldiers, saying, "Tell them, 'His disciples came at night and stole Him away while we slept.' And if this comes to the governor's ears, we will appease him and make you secure." So they took the money and did as they were instructed (Matthew 28:12-15a).

Even if the chief priests and Pharisees did not believe Jesus, they certainly understood what His promise meant. "After three days I will rise again." Their treachery had succeeded in having Him killed. They had made sure He was secured in the grave. They had asked for guards because they feared it might be hard to keep Him there. The chief priests, being Sadducees, denied any supernatural possibilities. The Pharisees differed doctrinally because they believed in the supernatural, including the possibility of resurrections. The fear they shared in this case, however, was that something—anything—might happen that would reassert Jesus' influence among the people. The missing body required quick action before word spread among the people. The people knew Jesus was a miracle worker. They knew He had been crucified. His burial was public knowledge. When the people learned the body was gone, the promise of His resurrection likely would be believed. Their desperation concocted a ludicrous and self-defeating solution. The more widely it was told, the more it would be known that the body was missing. Its weakest link was in the soldiers' admission of criminal dereliction. Could soldiers really explain how they had seen what they said they could not see?

This was the first of numerous attempts by unbelievers, ancient and modern, to explain away the facts. It should be noted that there was no denial that Jesus had been buried there. Neither has there ever been a credible claim that His body has been found. When Matthew wrote years later, the priests' ridiculous falsehood was still being told. There is wonderful irony, therefore, in that a lie intended to cover the facts is actually an admission of facts that speak for themselves. The tomb being empty and the body missing would become part of the compelling historical evidence of Christ's resurrection. Its importance is not simply that a grave was empty, but that it was His grave!

We do not know whether any of the guards ever became believers in Christ. The record says "some" of them came to report to the chief priests, possibly suggesting that all may not have agreed to the same report. When later they heard the ridiculous rumor, might they not have reflected seriously on the meaning of what actually happened? Their experience could hardly have been forgotten. In only a few weeks Jerusalem would be filled with the apostles' explanation of what had actually happened.

Did the Jewish leaders doubt the veracity of the guards' report?

Would we suppose they went to see for themselves?

Did they expect that the public would learn what had happened?

How did the priests' reaction show their panic?

First Announcement (Matthew 28:1-8; Mark 16:1-8; Luke 24:1-8; John 20:1)

In the early dawn of that Sunday morning, the women who had been so careful to know how and where Jesus was buried made their way back to the garden in hopes of adding more spices and perfumes. Mary Magdalene and Mary, the mother of Joses, and other women had stayed and watched until the heavy stone had been rolled into place. Among others coming to the garden were Salome, the mother of James and John, and Joanna (Mark 15:40-41; 16:1; Matthew 28:1; Luke 24:10). These women had been disciples and supporters of Jesus during His ministry and had been with the company that came with Him from Galilee. They had watched His suffering and death and had followed Joseph and Nicodemus to the grave to watch His burial.

Through the Sabbath they had rested in keeping with the law. Now at the beginning of the new day, they were coming to anoint the body with more spices. Assuming everything would still be in place, and with no men accompanying them, they wondered how the heavy stone could be moved. They seemed unaware of the stationing of Roman sentries, and that by the authority of the governor the tomb had been sealed, making it unlawful to be opened.

It was still dark in the shadows of the garden when Mary found the grave open. Apparently, instead of waiting to go inside with the others, she ran on to find Peter and John. This is assumed because it does not appear that she was with the others to hear the angel's announcement. They are astonished finding the stone moved and the crypt open. Inside the body was gone. Suddenly, their perplexity turned into astonishment as before them stood two men in dazzling white apparel. Luke mentions two angels, but Matthew and Mark tell only of the one spokesman. Critics have supposed contradictions in the different references to the angels, but regardless of how many were seen or whether they were standing or seated, the point is that angels made the first announcement of Christ's resurrection to these godly women. Terrified, they bowed their faces to the ground. Here are the angels' words as recorded in the synoptics:

> "Do not be afraid, for I know that you seek Jesus who was crucified. He is not here; for He is risen, as He said. Come, see the place where the Lord lay. And go quickly and tell His disciples that He is risen from the dead, and indeed He is going before you into Galilee; there you will see Him. Behold, I have told you" (Matthew 28:5-7).

> "Do not be alarmed. You seek Jesus of Nazareth, who was crucified. He is risen! He is not here. See the place where they laid Him. But go, tell His disciples — and Peter — that He is going before you into Galilee; there you will see Him, as He said to you" (Mark 16:6-7).

> "Why do you seek the living among the dead? He is not here, but is risen! Remember how He spoke to you when He was still in Galilee, saying, 'The Son of Man must be delivered into the hands of sinful men, and be crucified, and the third day rise again'" (Luke 24:5-7)

The announcement is brief, yet all the essentials are included.
- They said there was nothing to fear.
- They confirmed that they were at the right tomb, "Come see the place where the Lord lay."

- They assured that the One who had been buried there was Jesus of Nazareth.
- They affirmed that He had died by crucifixion.
- They affirmed that it was the third day since Jesus had died.
- They declared that Jesus was no longer dead, that He had risen.
- They reminded that Jesus had foretold these things before leaving Galilee.
- They instructed that the disciples, including Peter, be told and that as He had promised they would meet with Him in Galilee.

We may wonder why these women were chosen to hear the angels' message. An obvious answer is that they were the first to go to the sepulcher. Soon, they would actually see Jesus. It is noteworthy that women were the first eyewitnesses of the three foundation events of the gospel — Christ's death, burial, and resurrection. Only a few women heard that declaration, but the sound rings through the ages. There is no sepulcher where lies our Lord. Graves are for dead men. He is not dead. "He is risen!" The tomb is empty!

Can there be reasonable doubt as to the women going to the right tomb?

. . . .

Though the angel's announcements are brief, how do they match and confirm many other details concerning Christ's death and resurrection?

CHAPTER FOUR

He Is Risen, As He Said

WHEN THE ANGELS AT THE TOMB TOLD THE WOMEN CHRIST had risen, they reminded that this was "as He said" and told them to: "Remember how He spoke to you when He was still in Galilee, saying, 'The Son of Man must be delivered into the hands of sinful men, and be crucified, and the third day rise again" (Matthew 28:6; Luke 24:6-7).

Not only had the resurrection happened, it had been specifically predicted by the Lord Himself. It is not unusual for persons to make predictions. Such are a part of everyday life. Some have gained notability by having foretold certain major events with remarkable accuracy. In fact, however, those who tout themselves as prognosticators are wrong more often than right. What makes all of Jesus' predictions unique is His unfailing accuracy every time in every detail. His were not guesses. Neither were they left to alternative interpretation. Of the things He said, none is more specific than the pledge of His resurrection, even specifying that it would be on "the third day." Jesus Christ is not the only person who ever promised to come back after death, but He is the only person who ever did! That His resurrection was precisely foretold is as truly supernatural as the event itself.

Temple Prediction (John 2:13-22)

Early in the first year of His public ministry, Jesus went to the temple at the time of Passover and drove out the merchants and money changers. He had been to the temple many times, but on that occasion, He had gone to confront the religious aristocracy on their own ground.

> And He found in the temple those who sold oxen and sheep and doves, and the money changers doing business. When He had made a whip of cords, He drove them all out of the temple, with the sheep and the oxen, and poured out the changers' money and overturned the tables. And He said to those who sold doves, "Take these things away! Do not make My Father's house a house of merchandise!" Then His disciples remembered that it was written, "Zeal for Your house has eaten Me up" (John 2:14-17).

Passover was the first of the Law's required festivals. Thousands of Jewish pilgrims came from many lands. Among the requirements was the necessity of every household providing a proper sacrifice, which might be either brought with them or purchased after they arrived. Since temple contributions should be in the coinage of Judah, travelers could have their foreign money exchanged for a fee. Unscrupulous vendors, with the consent of the rulers, had set up a bazaar inside the temple court, selling oxen, sheep, and doves and charging exorbitant fees to exchange currency. That this holy place had become so crassly commercial was justified by its convenience and profitability. Jesus shut down the commerce.

The Jews protested, "What sign do You show to us, since You do these things? " (v. 18). They demanded proof of His authority, challenging Him to do something extraordinary or miraculous. He had, of course, just declared His authority. It was the authority of being right. The temple cleansing itself should have been sign enough. Whether they realized it or not, He was asserting His Messiahship. The temple was "My Father's house."

"Jesus answered and said to them, 'Destroy this temple, and in three days I will raise it up'" (v. 19). Here, in figurative language, was His first resurrection promise. At the time, the metaphor was not understood. His critics insisted on literalness. "It took forty-six years to build it, but this man says to destroy it and He can rebuild it in three days" (v. 20). It was not until all was fulfilled that even His disciples realized its meaning.

- The temple was His body, i.e., His life in the flesh. "The Word became flesh, and dwelt among us" (John 1:14).
- His enemies would "destroy" it by having Him crucified.
- "I will raise it up." As the Son of God, Deity Himself, He would raise Himself. A few others would be raised from death (e.g., Lazarus), but none by their own power.
- Though connected with a metaphor, the promise is exact regarding the time between the destroying (His death) and the rebuilding (His resurrection). It would be "in three days," a point expressed in similar words in other texts: "the third day," "after three days," "three days and three nights."

Whether Jesus repeated the temple reference on other occasions, it was a statement His enemies continued to hold in contempt. It would be one of the charges at His trial and repeated in the crowd's scornful mocking at the cross (Mark 14:59). Regardless, the rulers understood and feared "the third day" (Matthew 27:62-64).

Is a temple a fitting symbol of a person's fleshly life?

. . . .

In what way did Jesus imply His Messiahship?

Analogy with Jonah (Matthew 12:38-41; 16:4; Luke 11:29)

All Jesus' miraculous works were "signs" that corroborated His being sent from God. The religious hierarchy, however, were never satisfied and demanded to see more.

> Then some of the scribes and Pharisees answered, saying, "Teacher, we want to see a sign from You." But He answered and said to them, "An evil and adulterous generation seeks after a sign, and no sign will be given to it except the sign of the prophet Jonah. For as Jonah was three days and three nights in the belly of the great fish, so will the Son of Man be three days and three nights in the heart of the earth. The men of Nineveh will rise up in the judgment with this generation and condemn it, because they repented at the preaching of Jonah; and indeed a greater than Jonah is here"
> (Matthew 12:38-41).

Jesus did many "miracles, wonders, and signs," but He knew none would be sufficient for hearts so hardened. There was coming, however, one sign that would be proof above all proofs. He described it as "the sign of the prophet Jonah" (Matthew 12:39, 16:4, Luke 11:29).

Few things have been subjected to more ridicule by skeptics than the story of Jonah. Here, Jesus not only gives credibility to its historicity, but also applies it as an analogy of His own burial and resurrection. The prophet had been directed to preach to the heathen city Nineveh. Attempting to escape this duty, he boarded a ship bound for Tarshish. During a terrible storm, he was thrown overboard and swallowed by a great fish. He remained in the belly of the fish for "three days and three nights" before being vomited onto dry land. He was sent again to preach in Nineveh, and the result was the repentance of the whole city (Jonah 1-3).

The most casual reader knows that from any natural consideration Jonah could not have survived the fish experience. It is impossible in nature's laws that a human being could be swallowed by any kind of fish (sea creature, monster), survive three days and nights, and be vomited alive onto dry ground. It also seems beyond human expectations that Jonah's preaching would bring hundreds of thousands of Ninevites to repentance. But to believe in Jesus is to believe He always spoke truth. His own credibility authenticates the historical account of Jonah's story.

The Ninevites gave heed to Jonah's preaching because they were convinced that there was something unique about Jonah. The miracle that authenticated him as a prophet was in his experience with the fish. They did not see it happen, but by some means, they knew his remarkable story. A guess might be that the sailors who threw him overboard spread the news, and others had repeated it all the way to Nineveh. Regardless, somehow after his deliverance from the depths, they had realized that this prophet from Israel was under the care and guidance of the Almighty. Jonah was a "sign" to them. It was not necessary that the Ninevites see the miracle themselves, only that they believed what they heard. This point is important because it compares to the fact that we do not need to see Christ's death and resurrection to believe it. We know it happened because we believe the message we have heard. "So, then faith comes by hearing, and hearing by the word of God" (Romans 10:17).

In Jesus' analogy, the fish's belly corresponds to His grave, the three days and nights to the time of His entombment "in the heart of the earth." As Jonah was completely enclosed (out of sight) in the sea creature, so Jesus would be buried out of sight in the ground. A believer's complete immersion in baptism ("buried with Christ") is reminiscent of Jesus' burial being a complete enclosure (Romans 6:4; Colossians 2:12).

> *Did Jesus regard the story of Jonah as accurate history?*
>
> . . . .
>
> *How were the Ninevites convinced to heed Jonah's warning?*
>
> . . . .
>
> *Why did Jesus say no sign would be given except the sign He compared to Jonah?*

Plain Language (Matthew 16:17-23; Mark 8:31-33; Luke 9:22)

Wisdom understands that it is sometimes necessary to wait for an opportune time to reveal surprising and startling information. Early in His ministry, Jesus kept much in reserve about Himself. It would not be until the last year that He would begin to speak in plain words about His coming death and resurrection. He had spoken of it in the figure of a temple and in a comparison with the story of Jonah. It was not, however, until the disciples were sufficiently sure of His Messiahship that He could begin to tell them plainly about His forthcoming passion and victory.

> "Jesus had known from the beginning what would be the climax of His ministry."

They were together in the outskirts of Caesarea Philippi when Jesus asked the 12, "Who do men say that I, the Son of Man, am?" (Matthew 16:13). Their answer cited various confused opinions among the people. Then Jesus asked about their own convictions. Simon Peter, possibly intending to be spokesman for the rest, had confessed, "You are the Christ, the Son of the living God" (Matthew 16:16). Jesus assured Peter that what he had confessed was as certain as that "you are Peter." Then He declared that the truth of Peter's confession is the "rock" upon which "I will build my church and the gates of Hades [death] shall not prevail against it" (Matthew 16:18). Their loyalty was now sufficiently strong that Jesus could speak plainly about what they must anticipate.

> From that time Jesus began to show to His disciples that He must go to Jerusalem, and suffer many things from the elders and chief priests and scribes, and be killed, and be raised the third day. Then Peter took Him aside and began to rebuke Him, saying, "Far be it from You, Lord; this shall not happen to You!" But He turned and said to Peter, "Get behind Me, Satan! You are an offense to Me, for you are not mindful of the things of God, but the things of men" (Matthew 16:21-23).

It is not unusual for people to absorb only part of a traumatic announcement. From Peter's response, we get the impression that he, and probably the others, stopped listening after Jesus said He was going to be killed. That One so great as their Master might come to so ignominious an end was inconceivable. We may feel some sympathy for Peter's shocked reaction, but Jesus saw all as part of God's scheme of redemption.

> *Why had Jesus waited until His last year of ministry to speak plainly about His death and resurrection?*
>
> . . . .
>
> *Does it seem Peter did not realize that Jesus' prediction included a promise?*
>
> . . . .
>
> *Why would the gates of Hades be unable to prevail against the church?*

Still Confused
(Matthew 17:1-9;
Mark 9:10-11; Luke 9:28-36)

Leaving the area of Caesarea Philippi, they traveled to a high mountain, where Jesus took Peter, James, and John onto the mountain to pray. It was there that they witnessed His transfigured glory and saw with Him Moses and Elijah, "who appeared in glory and spoke of His decease which He was about to accomplish at Jerusalem."

Hastily, and without understanding, Peter wanted to make a permanent dwelling place with Jesus and the prophets. But immediately a cloud overshadowed them with a voice out of the cloud saying, "This is My beloved Son, in whom I am well pleased. Hear Him!" In times past God spoke "by the prophets," now speaks "by His Son" (Hebrews 1:1-2).

About what did Moses and Elijah communicate with Jesus?

. . . .

How does this and other examples of the disciples' confusion show that the resurrection story could not have been something the apostles contrived?

. . . .

Was it contrary to Jesus' prohibition when Peter later wrote about the transfiguration?

Coming down from the mountain, Jesus charged them to tell no one of the vision "until the Son of Man is risen from the dead" (Matthew 17:9). They understood the restriction and refrained from telling others. We can only guess at what must have been the total conversation between the three, but they seemed most puzzled over what He meant about "rising from the dead." Their inability to understand underscores the unlikelihood that later they might invent the resurrection story. Years later, however, Peter would write of being eyewitness of Christ's majesty and hearing the voice of God (2 Peter 2:16).

Another Time in Galilee (Matthew 17:22; Mark 9:31; Luke 9:43)

Not long after this, while still in Galilee, He tried to impress upon their minds the reality of what was soon to happen, "Let these words sink into your ears." (Luke 9:44). This was the second of three announcements in which He would speak bluntly about what was to happen. It was about six months before His crucifixion, and He was privately preparing them. Though His words may seem clear from our vantage, to them it was too unthinkable to grasp.

> "The Son of Man is being betrayed into the hands of
> men, and they will kill Him. And after He is killed, He
> will rise the third day." But they did not understand this
> saying, and were afraid to ask Him (Mark 9:31-32).

More Specific on Jerusalem Road (Matthew 20:17-19; Mark 10:32-34; Luke 18:31-34)

Jesus had known from the beginning what would be the climax of
His ministry. He had earlier foretold it by metaphor and analogy,
later by specific predictions. Now, as they neared Jerusalem, He
took the Twelve aside and reiterated the solemn announcement
with even more detail. He wanted to impress more forcefully that
all which was about to happen had been foretold through the
prophets and was in the purposes of God.

> Behold, we are going up to Jerusalem, and the Son
> of Man will be betrayed to the chief priests and to
> the scribes; and they will condemn Him to death and
> deliver Him to the Gentiles; and they will mock Him,
> and scourge Him, and spit on Him, and kill Him. And
> the third day He will rise again (Mark 10:33-34).

Only divine foreknowledge could describe exactly the coming
sequence of events. All except His resurrection would be at the
hands of others. One might be accurate in predicting things He
expected Himself to do. Here, however, Jesus was specifying
actions that would be taken by others. It would be Judas' choice
to betray Him. Soldiers would come to arrest Him. It would be
the Council's decision to indict Him. He would be "delivered" to

Why is it significant that many of the things He predicted would involve the actions of others?

. . . .

What are the various specifics given in all His predictions?

. . . .

Which of the things foretold might the disciples have believed might really happen?

the Gentiles (Romans), by whom He would be shamefully abused, tortured, and killed. All would happen shortly in Jerusalem. The third day after their murderous work was done, He would come back to life.

It cannot be missed that in spite of the plainness of Jesus' words, His disciples could not comprehend or believe. If they could not believe that such treachery and murder were about to occur, how much less could they conceive that afterward, He could come back to life.

Upper Room (John 16:16-22)

Five chapters in John's narrative (13-17) are about the Last Supper in the upper room. On the following afternoon, Jesus would die. Knowing this, He discoursed on many topics, trying to prepare them for the horrendous events about to unfold. They had been told in specific words about His death and resurrection. At that time, He spoke of what would be their experience. "A little while, and you will not see Me; and again a little while, and you will see Me, because I go to the Father" (John 16:16). In a short time, only hours away, He would die and be gone from their sight. Yet in another "little time" they would see Him again. This little time would be the three days of which Jesus spoke so often.

In less than 24 hours, they would see Him publicly, shamefully, and cruelly murdered. Jesus knew the heart-rending grief they were soon to endure. They were unprepared for the loss of their Master in any circumstance, made more unspeakable by the horror of seeing Him crucified. By the next afternoon, He would be gone. But that would not be the end of the story.

"Most assuredly, I say to you that you will weep and lament, but the world will rejoice; and you will be sorrowful, but your sorrow will be turned into joy.
A woman, when she is in labor, has sorrow because her hour has come; but as soon as she has given birth to the child, she no longer remembers the anguish, for joy that a human being has been born into the world. Therefore you now have sorrow; but I will see you again and your heart will rejoice, and your joy no one will take from you" (John 16:20-22).

In all these predictions, how confident was Jesus as to what would be the final outcome?

. . . .

Why are these predictions important in strengthening our faith in the resurrection?

CHAPTER FIVE

That Same Day

THE BODY OF JESUS HAD COME BACK TO LIFE EARLY ON THE first day of the week (our Sunday). This was the third day since He had been crucified. Because the angels had emphasized that Jesus had promised His own resurrection, we stepped back from the story to recall several times when He had foretold it. Now, we return to the narrative with other events on the first Lord's Day.

> "They have taken away the Lord out of the tomb, and
> we do not know where they have laid Him" (John 20:2).

Mary did not enter the tomb with the other women. It appears she may have arrived ahead of the others and, finding the stone door removed, hurried on to tell Peter and John. She had not heard the angels' announcement, nor was she thinking about Jesus' promise to arise. She only knew something was amiss at the grave.

She saw the stone had been moved. She assumed the Lord's body had been carried away. She was not bringing good news of the resurrection, but shock over His missing body. The news sent Peter and John running to see for themselves. Luke only mentions Peter going, but in John's account, he ran faster and arrived first. (John does not identify himself by name, but as the author of the book, calls himself "the disciple whom Jesus loved.") He stooped to look inside, but waited for Peter to enter first. Mary was right! The grave was open, and Jesus was gone.

> And he [John], stooping down and looking in, saw the linen cloths lying there; yet he did not go in. Then Simon Peter came, following him, and went into the tomb; and he saw the linen cloths lying there, and the handkerchief that had been around His head, not lying with the linen cloths, but folded together in a place by itself. Then the other disciple, who came to the tomb first, went in also; and he saw and believed. For as yet they did not know the Scripture, that He must rise again from the dead. Then the disciples went away again to their own homes (John 20:5-10).

Even from outside, he could see the cloths in which Jesus had been wrapped. Then inside, the significance of the scene began to register in his mind. There was no body, only the clothing in His place. The separate piece of material that had covered His head was folded and lying in a place by itself. Jesus had put aside the shroud bandages and made His departure. The living Lord had no need for the clothing of the dead.

If human hands had carried Him away, they would have taken no time to unwrap the linen cloths. Even if they had, the pieces would have been left crumpled and scattered. The orderly arrangement inside the chamber belied the guards' story. If disciples had taken the body in the darkness with the guards nearby, it would have been nonsensical to remove the wrappings and fold the head piece. Not only that, as Peter and John were prominent among the disciples, they would have known of any plot to steal the corpse.

The same improbability applies to any suggestion that others had robbed the grave. Of course, if robbers had taken Him, the chief priests would readily have paid a ransom. Countered too is the so-called "swoon theory." Aside from the overwhelming proof of His death, the problem of the heavy stone, the presence of the guards, and other obstacles: What purpose would one in such a condition have for removing His bandages, folding the face towel, and struggling naked out of the ground? Instead, the bandages had been removed by the same power by which He had walked on water, stilled the storm, and multiplied bread and fish. He left all in place for these disciples to see. The details John gives attest to their careful scrutiny.

John confesses that in seeing these things, he came to believe. It was no longer an issue of a missing body. No search was going to be initiated because they knew a corpse would never be found. They returned to their homes and reported what they had seen. As John later wrote of these things, he humbly admitted that what these signs proved was what they should have already known from Scripture.

Nothing more is said in the Bible about the pieces of cloth, nor about them being preserved as holy relics. In the late Medieval Ages, claims began to be made of the discovery of a sheet that was supposed to be the actual cloth that had covered Jesus' body: the "Shroud of Turin." The claim is that there are impressions of wound marks in the material that would be caused by crucifixion. It cannot be proven that it dates from the first century, and even if it appears to have marks consistent with crucifixion, there is no proof that the victim was Jesus. Though there has been much excitement in some circles about this "sacred" relic, the claims do not match the details of Scripture. In the first place, instead of a single covering from head to feet, a separate cloth covered the face. Further, the Bible speaks of cloths (plural). No mention is made of a single covering for the whole body (John 20:6f). The Shroud, like other supposed relics associated with Christ, may intrigue those who revel in superstitions, but our faith is in the inspired history of Holy Scripture.

> *How can it be explained that Mary did not hear the angels' announcement before reporting to Peter and John?*
>
> . . . .
>
> *At this point does it appear that neither Mary or Peter and John were hopeful, only perplexed?*
>
> . . . .
>
> *Why would the cloth wrappings and face cloth be of any significance?*

The First to See Him (John 20:11-18; Mark 16:9-11)

According to Mark, Mary Magdalene was the first to actually see the risen Lord (Mark 16:9). Only John gives details of that meeting. She was among several women in Galilee who had been faithful followers of Christ from early in His ministry. She is distinguished from the others by the exceptional miracle, which freed her from seven demons. Contrary to scandalous notions advanced by some, there is no evidence that she had once been a prostitute or that she had been married to Jesus. Such notions are the product of profane minds. Neither is she to be confused with the sinful woman who had once washed Jesus' feet with her tears, nor with the Mary who anointed Him in Bethany. What is true is that she was among the last at the cross and was the first to see Him alive. It is interesting that the first appearance of the risen Lord was to Mary, not to the apostles, and that it was not the Mary who was His mother. (There is no evidence that the resurrected Jesus ever appeared to His mother.)

Peter and John were gone by the time she came back to the garden. Whether on her way back she came into contact with the two apostles is not known. In her anguish, the possibility of Jesus being alive was not imagined. His body was missing, and she wanted to find it. Perplexed and weeping, she stooped to look into the tomb. "And she saw two angels in white sitting, one at the head and the other at the feet where the body had lain. Then they said to her, "Woman, why are you weeping?" (John 20:12-13).

Why weeping? Why indeed? The One she loved above all others had been betrayed by His friend, forsaken by His followers, and cruelly murdered by His enemies. Now, even the opportunity to mourn beside Him had been taken away. Even the presence of angels does not assuage her grief.

> She said to them, "Because they have taken away my Lord, and I do not know where they have laid Him." Now when she had said this, she turned around and saw Jesus standing there, and did not know that it was Jesus. Jesus said to her, "Woman, why are you weeping? Whom are you seeking?" She, supposing Him to be the gardener, said to Him, "Sir, if You have carried Him away, tell me where You have laid Him, and I will take Him away." Jesus said to her, "Mary!" (John 20:13-16).

What emotions must have flooded her heart — what surprise! What mixture of belief and wonder! What joy! This was her Master's voice.

> She turned and said to Him, "Rabboni!" (which is to say, Teacher). Jesus said to her, "Do not cling to Me, for I have not yet ascended to My Father; but go to My brethren and say to them, 'I am ascending to My Father and your Father, and to My God and your God'" (John 20:16-17).

The brevity of this exchange leaves several questions and prompted various explanations. What we know for sure is that Mary could now be certain He is alive.

We know, however, that there was nothing inherently wrong about touching Him because soon He would allow others to do so. The Greek tense indicates that He was telling her to stop what she was doing. Was she clinging to Him to be sure He was really there (and not a mere apparition), or was she wanting to prolong their being together? She called Him "Rabboni," which may imply she was thinking their former relationship as Teacher and disciple could now be restored.

Jesus intended for her to take a message to "My brethren." That they were His "brethren" is underscored in "My Father" being also "your Father." Jesus is uniquely the Son of God. All who serve Him are also children of God and brothers and sisters of Christ (1 John 3:1-2). His disciples had failed Him greatly, but His affection was not diminished. He "is not ashamed to call them brethren" (Hebrews 2:11-12).

His statements about having "not yet ascended" and "I am ascending" indicate both a present and a future fact. The present fact was to assure Mary that not only was He alive, but that He was there. He had not yet gone to heaven, but alive in the flesh and still on the earth. In Mary's case, as well as all the others, His appearances were not visions, but His actual living body in the flesh.

The time would come when He would ascend out of this world, but He had not ascended yet. Thus, she was to tell His brethren: "I am ascending," which would reaffirm what He had explained many times. "I came forth from the Father, and am come into the world: again, I leave the world, and go to the Father" (John 16:28). This pointed to when He would be taken up in Acts 1:9. His statement might be paraphrased: "I am really here now; I have not yet ascended; but the time will come when I will ascend."

Jesus had told the penitent thief, "Assuredly, I say to you, today you will be with Me in Paradise" (Luke 23:43). By comparing that with the text before us, it is evident that His reference to "Paradise" was not heaven, the eternal home with the Father, but instead the temporary abode of righteous spirits. While His body lay in the grave, His Spirit had been in the paradise realm of the spirit world. He had come back from the spirit world. He had not yet ascended to heaven, but at the proper time He would.

What stands out with certainty is that Mary is the first eyewitness to see Jesus alive and the first to tell the good news. This time it was not to report a missing body. Now it was, "I have seen the Lord." Mark says that when she reported this to the grieving apostles, they did not believe her. This does not mean that they would never believe her, as is evident in this record given by John.

How does Mark identify which Mary was first to see the risen Lord?

. . . .

Did Jesus mean He was going to ascend immediately?

The Second Appearance (Matthew 28:9-10)

The Scriptures do not dwell on the resurrection event itself, but on how Jesus made Himself known to various followers. They would see Him, be assured that indeed it was He, and know He is alive. These appearances are the "proofs" that convinced the eyewitnesses to testify to the world that "Christ died and rose and lived again, that He might be Lord of both the dead and the living" (Romans 14:9).

Much was happening at about the same time in the early hours of the day. Peter and John had gone to the tomb. Mary had seen the Lord. Other women, who trembling with joy, astonishment, and fear, had heard the angels' announcement and were on their way to tell the apostles. Much was on their minds about having seen and heard the heavenly messengers and in remembering things Jesus had earlier said about coming back to life.

Along the way, they may have passed strangers, even friends, but spoken to no one. As the apostles may have been staying in different places and as there were different routes, they likely would encounter John, Peter, or Mary.

> And as they went to tell His disciples, behold, Jesus met them, saying, "Rejoice!" So they came and held Him by the feet and worshiped Him. Then Jesus said to them, "Do not be afraid. Go *and* tell My brethren to go to Galilee, and there they will see Me" (Matthew 28:9-10).

They brought the greatest news of the greatest story ever told, but to the men it was too good to be true. "And their words seemed to them like idle tales, and they did not believe them" (Luke 24:11). It need not be assumed that all the women found all the brethren at the same time. Luke's statement which lists all the women, including Mary Magdalene, does not preclude Mary having given a separate report. It is only a summary of how the various reports were first received.

Mary and these women were eyewitnesses to the three greatest events in the history of the world, the events that are the foundation of the gospel message. They saw Him die. They saw Him buried. They saw Him living again. In those times, the testimony of women would not have been as credible as that of men. If the story of the resurrection were made up, it is unlikely a fiction writer would have cast women as the first to see Him.

> *How does the women being named as the first to see Jesus add to the credibility of the record?*
>
> . . . .
>
> *Is it reasonable that their report was not readily believed?*

Privately to Peter (1 Corinthians 15:5; Luke 24:34)

Only two references tell of Peter seeing Christ before He was seen by the other apostles. Years afterward, when Paul gave a partial list of eyewitnesses of the risen Lord, he named Peter as the first apostle to have seen Him. "He was seen by Cephas [Simon Peter], then of the twelve" (1 Corinthians 15:5). "The twelve" is a term used for the apostolic group, though only 10 were present when Christ first appeared to the group. The other reference is in the report that would be given later to Cleopas and his companion. When they found the apostles gathered in

> "Mary is the first eyewitness to see Jesus alive and the first to tell the good news."

Jerusalem they were told, "The Lord is risen indeed, and has appeared to Simon!" (Luke 24:34).

Neither Luke nor Paul gives details about the appearance to Peter. It was sometime during the same day after Peter and John had visited the empty tomb and after the appearance to Mary. No explanation is given as to why Peter was given this privilege ahead of the others. Some have supposed it was to assure him that in spite of his having thrice denied the Lord, he was not less loved. It also may have been because he had so often had been a leading voice in the apostolic group. It was not, as some have argued, to assure him a place of primacy in the church (i.e., as pope).

What are the only two references to a private meeting with Simon Peter?

. . . .

Were the others convinced Peter had seen the resurrected Lord?

On the Emmaus Road (Luke 24:13-35; Mark 16:12)

Later in the afternoon that first Lord's Day, two disciples left Jerusalem and were walking toward a village called Emmaus, which was about seven miles from Jerusalem. These were not of the Twelve. One was named Cleopas. (Though the names are similar, this was not the Clopas of John 19:25.) Nothing more is known about Cleopas, and there is no hint of the identity of his companion.

Theirs was no casual conversation. The mood of Jesus' followers was much different from what would be expected if the story concocted by the priests had been true. While they sadly talked of the events that had transpired, Jesus joined them and asked, "What kind of conversation is this that you have with one another as you walk and are sad?" They were prevented from recognizing Him.

> Then the one whose name was Cleopas answered and
> said to Him, "Are You the only stranger in Jerusalem,
> and have You not known the things which happened
> there in these days?" "What things?" Jesus asked.
> So they said to Him, "The things concerning Jesus of
> Nazareth, who was a Prophet mighty in deed and
> word before God and all the people, and how the
> chief priests and our rulers delivered Him to be con-
> demned to death, and crucified Him. But we were
> hoping that it was He who was going to redeem Israel.
> Indeed, besides all this, today is the third day since
> these things happened. Yes, and certain women of our
> company, who arrived at the tomb early, astonished
> us. When they did not find His body, they came saying
> that they had also seen a vision of angels who said He
> was alive. And certain of those who were with us went
> to the tomb and found it just as the women had said;
> but Him they did not see (Luke 24:18-24).

They wanted to tell everything they knew about Jesus: the horrendous injustice inflicted on Him, the spectacle of Calvary, His hours of
passionate suffering, and even the puzzling reports about the empty
tomb and missing body. All of this would overwhelm the emotions of
those who had so loved and trusted Him. As we reflect on His passion,
we have our own degree of pathos about it. Because we know the
glorious end of the story, our empathy may be limited, but for Cleopas
and his friend there had not been time to adjust to the shock and confusion of recent days and hours. They left Jerusalem and the company
of the apostles in sad bewilderment. Only one topic — a topic full of
questions — could be their conversation as they walked toward home.

Though there was uncertainty about the reports of His having risen, there was no doubt about the reality of His death. They explained, "But we were hoping that it was He who was going to redeem Israel" (Luke 24:21), which was to say hope was gone. It was difficult to believe in the resurrection because they could not understand the necessity of His death. They could not see past the cross. Later, Paul would write of the world's contempt for the cross. "But we preach Christ crucified, to the Jews a stumbling block and to the Greeks foolishness, but to those who are called, both Jews and Greeks, Christ the power of God and the wisdom of God" (1 Corinthians 1:23-24). These men and all the others did not understand that He could not be the Saving Sovereign without first being the Suffering Servant.

> Then He said to them, "O foolish ones, and slow of heart
> to believe in all that the prophets have spoken! Ought
> not the Christ to have suffered these things and to enter
> into His glory?" And beginning at Moses and all the
> Prophets, He expounded to them in all the Scriptures the
> things concerning Himself (Luke 24:25-27).

Still without revealing Himself, and without commenting directly on the events that so troubled them, Jesus rebuked them for their lack of understanding and confidence in the message of the prophets. "O foolish ones, and slow of heart to believe in all that the prophets have spoken!" Our translation has "foolish ones" (fools), but it is not the word that means wicked or contemptible (which in Matthew 5:22 we are forbidden to use). Rather it is a word that implied their slowness to grasp "all that the prophets have spoken!" Later, beginning on Pentecost, emphasis would be given to eye-witness testimony, but at this point, Jesus does not persuade them to believe because of the reports they have heard, but because of what they should have understood from the prophets. In contrast to the doubts of many today as to its inspiration and inerrancy, Jesus urged absolute trust in the revelations of Holy Scripture. This is a powerful reminder of the place of Scripture in the Divine scheme of things. New Testament preachers argued the case for Christ using proof texts of Scripture (e.g., Acts 17:2-3). All these things are "according to the Scriptures" (1 Corinthians 15:3-4).

> "If human hands had carried Him away, they would have taken no time to unwrap the linen cloths. Even if they had, the pieces would have been left crumpled and scattered."

This was the first time the redemption story in its fulfillment had been expounded. As the two men listened, their hearts burned with excitement. We are not told of any specific texts Jesus cited, but certain ones are likely to have been included, and each is worthy of careful study (e.g., Psalm 22; Psalm 16; Isaiah 53).

As they neared their destination, though assuming this stranger's intention was to go on, they invited Him to be their overnight guest. In Hebrews 13:2 Christians are encouraged "to entertain strangers, for by so doing some have unwittingly entertained angels." Cleopas and his friend did not know this stranger was actually the Son of God.

> Now it came to pass, as He sat at the table with them, that He took bread, blessed and broke it, and gave it to them. Then their eyes were opened and they knew Him; and He vanished from their sight. And they said to one another, "Did not our heart burn within us while He talked with us on the road, and while He opened the Scriptures to us?" (Luke 24:30-32).

They were about seven miles from Jerusalem, and it had been their intention to stay for the night. Instead, they hastened back to share their experience with the others. As it happened, fresh news also awaited them. When they had left Jerusalem, there were doubts and confusion. Now they found 10 of the apostles and others together in jubilant excitement. Before Cleopas and his friend could tell their own story, the greeting they received was, "The Lord is risen indeed, and has appeared to Simon!"

Just as John was the only writer to give details of the appearance to Mary Magdalene, so only Luke, except for a brief reference in Mark, records details of Jesus meeting these friends on the Emmaus road. The Holy Spirit's purpose was to record a variety of events that affirm the resurrection.

What did Jesus mean about "enter into His glory"?

What might have been the reason for Jesus' disappearing so quickly?

How did these brethren describe their emotional response to what they had come to understand?

CHAPTER SIX

Showed Himself to His Disciples

JOHN'S NARRATIVE DOES NOT MENTION CHRIST'S APPEAR-ances to the other women, or to Peter, or in the home at Emmaus. Instead, he moves from early in the day when Jesus appeared to Mary Magdalene to evening of the same day when He met with the apostles. Luke's account of Cleopas and his friend's return is continued with the Lord's appearance in the upper room. The apostles as a group had been known as "the twelve," but after the defection and death of Judas, both Mark and Luke identify the group as "the eleven." In fact, however, when Jesus came to them on that Lord's Day evening, only 10 of the original 12 were present. Thomas was not there. Others present may have included Matthias, who would later be added to the apostleship.

Much had happened in the morning hours of that first Lord's Day. By evening, the disciples must have known the story being told by the Roman guards and had reason to fear they might be arrested. They had closed themselves in for fear, but this is not John's only reason for stating the door was closed. Rather it was to underscore the supernatural way Jesus would enter. There was much to talk about: the empty grave; the burial bandages; what Mary, the other women, and even Peter said they saw. Now Cleopas and his friend had come to describe their experience. The atmosphere was a mixture of melancholy, belief, fear, doubt, excitement, and wonder. The empty tomb was a fact. Even the priests knew the body was missing. Evidence pointed to Jesus being alive. But could Peter and these women be sure it was really Jesus they had seen?

Suddenly their conversation was interrupted by Jesus appearing in their midst. He did not come through the door. They did not see Him walk into the room. He was just there. Here is one of the marvels of His resurrection form. He could be seen, heard, and touched. Yet walls, shrouds, tombs, and distances never were in the way. In Luke's account the Greek is emphatic: "Himself!" (i.e., "Jesus Himself"). He just was there, and said, "Peace be with you."

> But they were terrified and frightened, and supposed they had seen a spirit. And He said to them, "Why are you troubled? And why do doubts arise in your hearts? Behold My hands and My feet, that it is I Myself. Handle Me and see, for a spirit does not have flesh and bones as you see I have." When He had said this, He showed them His hands and His feet. But while they still did not believe for joy, and marveled, He said to them, "Have you any food here?" So they gave Him a piece of a broiled fish and some honeycomb. And He took it and ate in their presence (Luke 24:34-43).

He came to reprove them for slowness to believe what they had been told (Mark 16:14). They should have accepted it, not as hearsay, or hallucination, or unrealistic hope, but as confirmation of what Jesus had promised. The proof was there, and wonderful proof it was, but still hard to believe. Their joy in seeing Him struggled against what they thought impossible. His death had been too final. No corpse had ever brought itself back to life. They needed "many infallible proofs" (Acts 1:3). By such proofs, He was preparing them to be His witnesses, "to testify that it is He who was ordained by God to be Judge of the living and the dead" (Acts 10:42-43).

The wounds were visible. John adds that He showed them His side. Here was a living person in the flesh, but with open lacerations caused by crucifixion. The proof was tangible. Jesus asked for food and was given a piece of fish and honeycomb, which He ate as they watched. They needed to realize that He was a real person and the same person they had seen die three days before. His was a resurrected body, but it was indeed His body. In that He said, "a spirit does not have flesh and bones," we can logically infer it is possible one's spirit can exist outside the body. But Jesus was making the point that He was not a ghost!

Who was present in the room?

. . . .

How could they be happy and doubtful at the same time?

. . . .

In what ways did Jesus prove Himself to be real?

. . . .

What were some things revealed about His resurrected body?

His Ambassadors (John 20:21-23; 2 Corinthians 5:20)

> So Jesus said to them again, "Peace to you! As the
> Father has sent Me, I also send you." And when He
> had said this, He breathed on them, and said to them,
> "Receive the Holy Spirit. If you forgive the sins of any,
> they are forgiven them; if you retain the sins of any,
> they are retained" (John 20:21-23).

Though others were present, particular attention is given to His apostles. He was preparing them for their commission as His witnesses and representatives. The term apostle means someone commissioned to carry out an assigned mission. Also implied is requisite authority. The term is sometimes applied to others, but has special significance for the 11 (and later for Matthias and Paul). He said, "As the Father has sent Me, I also send you." They would be sent to preach, but to be more than preachers. They would have a special place of authority as "ambassadors of Christ" (2 Corinthians 5:20).

The term *ambassador* means an official representative of a head of state. The apostles would represent King Jesus after He returned to heaven. Thus, they had the delegated authority of Christ. Their message would be Christ's message. "Most assuredly, I say to you, he who receives whomever I send receives Me; and he who receives Me receives Him who sent Me" (John 13:20; see also Luke 10:16).

The focal point of this commission was the plan of salvation ("If you forgive the sins of any..."). Such would not be left to the apostles' (or any man's) personal discretion. Sin can be forgiven only by the Lord. The apostles' part would be to declare the basis upon which men and women could receive forgiveness. What this would involve in actual practice can be determined by comparing the other ways Jesus defined it and how the apostles carried it out. Other statements of this "Great Commission" are in Matthew 28, Mark 16, Luke 24, where requirements for forgiveness are specified. The conversion stories in Acts show these requirements as they were preached and believed.

When would the power of the Spirit actually come upon them?

. . . .

What is the significance of apostle *and* ambassador *as applied to the 10 in the upper room?*

. . . .

How can we know when and how their salvation ministry was put into practice?

Previously He had promised a Helper, the Holy Spirit, to be their guide "into all truth" (John 14:26, 16:13). In this meeting in the upper room, he symbolically renewed the promise by breathing on them and saying, "Receive the Holy Spirit." The promised Helper (Holy Spirit) would not come until after He ascended (John 16:7). He was pointing, therefore, to the day of Pentecost when they were filled with the Spirit and began preaching the Gospel plan of salvation (Luke 24:49; Act 1:8; Acts 2).

"After Eight Days"

On the first Lord's Day, there were five recorded occasions when he was seen by various of His followers. Nothing is said about how long He stayed that first evening or where He was and what He did for the rest of that week. During that week, however, the disciples found Thomas and gave the good news to him. We don't know when or where they had met with Thomas, but we can be sure they never neglected trying to persuade him. Neither do we know whether others were told during that week or whether any believed. We do know that the priests' false rumor was being spread through the city.

Then, as now, many hearing the gospel dismiss it with indifference or incredulity. In Thomas's case, however, it was not that he did not want to believe. To him the news simply seemed too wonderful to believe. The accumulated experience of mankind denied that a dead person could come back to life. Yes, Thomas knew there had been certain ones raised, but none had come back on their own, especially after such a brutal murder. Cruel spikes had torn through Jesus' hands and feet. His life blood had dripped to the ground. The Roman spear had left a gaping hole in His side. He knew no one could have survived such merciless and bloody crucifixion.

> "Here was a living person in the flesh, but with open lacerations caused by crucifixion. The proof was tangible."

Yet they were telling him his beloved Master three days later had been seen walking, talking, and eating. They claimed they had actually examined His wounds. They had watched Him eat a piece of fish. But Thomas said, "Unless I see in His hands the print of the nails, and put my finger into the print of the nails, and put my hand into His side, I will not believe" (John 20:25).

One of the most absurd theories proposed by some infidels is that Jesus had not really died, that He had only passed out (or pretended to be dead) and after reviving in the tomb had gotten out and started lying to people about being raised. That absurdity never entered Thomas's mind. The question to him was not whether Jesus was ever dead, but whether He is now alive. (Incidentally, though it is correctly understood that He had been nailed to the cross, this is the only place in the crucifixion narrative that nails are actually mentioned.)

Why was Thomas absent that previous Sunday night? Possibly he had already heard reports, but thought them so implausible that he did not want to be involved. From what we know about his life, neither his absence nor his hesitancy to believe should be construed as lack of devotion. He had not broken his ties with the other disciples. Whatever the cause of his earlier absence, at their gathering the following week, he was present. They were still in Jerusalem, possibly at the same place, when Jesus entered in the same supernatural way.

In what sense was Thomas a doubter?

. . . .

What are some different causes of doubt?

. . . .

Does his questioning indicate a weakness in his loyalty to Christ?

. . . .

Why did he demand the specific need to examine the wounds?

Thomas is sometimes denigrated as "Doubting Thomas." There is a difference between honest doubt and stubbornness. An honest doubter can be persuaded by reasonable evidence. So-called "blind faith" better describes superstition than Christianity. In fact, in many matters it is not wise simply to take the word of others. Conclusions cannot be fairly reached until facts are known. "Test all things; hold fast to what is good" (1 Thessalonians 5:21). On the other hand, a prejudiced mind that refuses to accept evidence will never know the truth.

For Himself (John 20:24-31)

Thomas's honesty becomes obvious as the narrative unfolds. The actuality of his initial unbelief should not be minimized. Jesus did not describe him as simply one who wanted to be sure, but rather as "unbelieving." It adds greatly to his credibility as a witness to realize the totality of his mind change. Unbelief gave way to the evidence and became dynamic faith.

> And after eight days His disciples were again inside, and Thomas with them. Jesus came, the doors being shut, and stood in the midst, and said, "Peace to you!" Then He said to Thomas, "Reach your finger here, and look at My hands; and reach your hand here, and put it into My side. Do not be unbelieving, but believing" (John 20:26-27).

It was more than an invitation. Thomas was told to do it. In other circumstances what Thomas had demanded and what Jesus welcomed would seem gruesome — reaching inside to feel the torn flesh and putting his finger into the holes made by the spikes. But the others had experienced touching Him, and Thomas needed the same. This was part of the verification that they were not seeing a spirit, that it was really Him (Luke 24:39). John would later reflect on the certainty of that "which we have heard, which we have seen with our eyes, which we have looked upon, and our hands have handled, concerning the Word of life" (1 John 1:1).

> "Thomas's honesty becomes obvious as the narrative unfolds… Unbelief gave way to the evidence and became dynamic faith."

It is useful to note that "after eight days" would mean the next Sunday, another first day of the week. All four Gospel narratives specify that Christ's resurrection was on the first day of the week. This second meeting with the apostles was also on a Sunday. The day of Pentecost, the day of the beginning of the church, was on a Sunday. Congregations met on Sundays to partake of the Lord's Supper (Acts 20:7) and to give their weekly contributions (1 Corinthians 16:1-2). In recognition that Christ arose, among Christians, Sunday came to be known as "the Lord's Day" (Revelation 1:10). Psalm 118:22-24 foresees Christ becoming the "chief cornerstone" by His resurrection and declares, "This is the day the Lord has made; We will rejoice and be glad in it."

What would be the purpose of touching the wounds?

. . . .

How careful is John to affirm that the Jesus who appeared to them was without question the same person as had died by crucifixion?

. . . .

What emphasis is given to the day of the week?

. . . .

How do we know the "stone" prophecy in Psalm 118 pointed to the resurrection?

The Good Confession

"My Lord and my God!" Though Thomas was the last of the Twelve (surviving 11) to believe, he was the first on record to address Him as Lord and God. This is not to be minimized as merely a surprise exclamation. It acknowledges fact.

Any doubt as to the appropriateness of his wording is answered by Jesus' immediate commendation and acceptance of it as a confession of his faith.

He recognized Christ's resurrection as proof of His deity. The "Son of God" is "God the Son." "For in Him dwells all the fullness of the Godhead bodily; and you are complete in Him, who is the head of all principality and power" (Colossians 2:9-10). Jesus is fully God and Lord in position and power.

What is acknowledged in the good confession is the fundamental proposition of Christianity. To believe in His literal resurrection is the beginning place of gospel obedience.

> [I]f you confess with your mouth the Lord Jesus and believe in your heart that God has raised Him from the dead, you will be saved. For with the heart one believes unto righteousness, and with the mouth confession is made unto salvation (Romans 10:9-10).

This brings us back to how Jesus commended Thomas. "Thomas, because you have seen Me, you have believed. Blessed are those who have not seen and yet have believed" (John 20:29). The apostles were eyewitnesses. The divine plan was for Thomas and the others to see for themselves. They had to be sure before they could give assurance to others. They could only testify as to what they knew firsthand. But what about those "who have not seen"? How do they/we come to believe? The answer is in the purpose John gives for writing the story.

Why is it significant to see that Thomas's confession was more than just an excited exclamation?

Is it possible to believe in Jesus without believing His body literally came back to life?

. . . .

What can we possibly know of these things without relying on the Scriptures?

. . . .

Does making the good confession involve more than making a statement?

And truly Jesus did many other signs in the presence of His disciples, which are not written in this book; but these are written that you may believe that Jesus is the Christ, the Son of God, and that believing you may have life in His name" (John 20:30-31).

CHAPTER SEVEN

Witnesses Chosen Before God

THE NEW TESTAMENT AFFIRMS CHRIST'S RESURRECTION AS essential doctrine and gives the evidence in proof thereof. Saving faith and obedience require that "you confess with your mouth the Lord Jesus and believe in your heart that God has raised Him from the dead..." (Romans 10:9). "In your heart" means fully persuaded with no reservations. Confession with the mouth is a work of obedience. What is spoken with the mouth is confessed in action when we are "**buried** with Him through baptism into death, that just as Christ was **raised** from the dead by the glory of the Father, even so we also should walk in newness of **life**" (Romans 6:4, emphasis added).

In our own age of somewhat comfortable Christianity, we marvel at the courage and endurance of faithful Christians in Bible times. Stephen is remembered for his unwavering faith even as stones crushed away his life (Acts 7:57-60).

A lesser-known martyr named Antipas held to faith in a city so evil that it was called Satan's dwelling place (Revelation 2:13). When warned about imprisonment in Jerusalem, Paul insisted on going anyway, saying, "For I am ready not only to be bound, but also to die at Jerusalem for the name of the Lord Jesus" (Acts 21:13). Years later imprisoned in Rome and facing execution his faith had not wavered. (See also 2 Timothy 4:6-7; Philippians 1:20-24; Revelation 12:11.)

It might be imagined that it was easier for people in the first century to have such courageous faith because they lived closer to the actual events. The fact is, however, that most Christians in New Testament times never saw Jesus in person. His ministry on earth was restricted to a narrow strip of land on the western coast of the Mediterranean. Though there were occasions when thousands gathered to see Him, those numbers pale to those who later would become believers in far distant lands.

More to the point is the minuscule number who were privileged to see Him after His resurrection. In 1 Corinthians 15:5-8 Paul gives a partial list of those to whom He appeared. In addition to these were Mary Magdalene, certain other women, and the two men with whom He walked on the road to Emmaus. All added together, the total who are known

> "We can know nothing about the life, death, and resurrection of Jesus except by the testimony in Scripture."

to have actually seen the resurrected Savior will be a few over 500. Paul names himself as the last one (1 Corinthians 15:8).

Yet it was their absolute certainty that Jesus is the risen Savior that caused early Christians to be willing to sacrifice everything, even their own lives, to maintain their conviction. This is the background of a significant statement Peter wrote to Christians scattered in various provinces of Asia Minor. They were facing a fiery trial and could expect to "suffer for righteousness' sake" (1 Peter 3:14; 4:12). They were not among the few who had known the Lord in person. Yet Peter describes their devotion to Christ:

Is it possible to be saved without being convinced that Jesus came back to life?

. . . .

What shows that Christians in the first century had such conviction?

. . . .

Did Jesus indicate that most believers would have an experience similar to that of Thomas?

Whom having not seen you love. Though now you do not see Him, yet believing, you rejoice with joy inexpressible and full of glory, receiving the end of your faith — the salvation of your souls (1 Peter 1:8-9).

Such believers were in view when Jesus said to Thomas: "Thomas, because you have seen Me, you have believed. Blessed are those who have not seen and yet have believed" (John 20:29).

"Not to All the People, but to Witnesses" (Acts 10:38-42)

The risen Lord Jesus was seen by the apostles for 40 days right up to and including His ascension. In this, He was preparing them to be His witnesses. The New Testament gives singular attention to their role as such. The term, *witnesses*, indicates their having seen and heard Him (eyewitnesses) and therefore qualified to give firsthand testimony.

> Then He said to them, "Thus it is written, and thus it was necessary for the Christ to suffer and to rise from the dead the third day, and that repentance and remission of sins should be preached in His name to all nations, beginning at Jerusalem. And you are witnesses of these things. Behold, I send the Promise of My Father upon you; but tarry in the city of Jerusalem until you are endued with power from on high" (Luke 24:45-49).

The same is reiterated in Acts 1:8. "But you shall receive power when the Holy Spirit has come upon you; and you shall be witnesses to Me in Jerusalem, and in all Judea and Samaria, and to the end of the earth." The resurrection story was to be validated by eyewitness testimony. This is emphasized in frequent references. "This Jesus God has raised up, of which we are all witnesses" (Acts 2:32). "[W]hom God raised from the dead, of which we are witnesses" (Acts 3:15). "And with great power the apostles gave witness to the resurrection of the Lord Jesus" (Acts 4:33). "And we are His witnesses to these things" (Acts 5:32). They were "eyewitnesses" in having literally seen Him. Peter gives this explanation in Acts 10:39-42:

In preaching Christ, why did the apostles emphasize that they were eyewitnesses?

. . . .

Can a person "witness" (testify) something about which he has no firsthand knowledge?

And we are witnesses of all things which He did both in the land of the Jews and in Jerusalem, whom they killed by hanging on a tree. Him God raised up on the third day, and showed Him openly, not to all the people, but to witnesses chosen before by God, *even* to us who ate and drank with Him after He arose from the dead. And He commanded us to preach to the people, and to testify that it is He who was ordained by God *to be* Judge of the living and the dead.

Were all the men and women who saw Jesus appointed to be His witnesses?

. . . .

Is there any sense in which Christians can be witnesses concerning Christ?

This is not to say that others (preachers, teachers, anyone) cannot repeat the testimony, but the actual witnesses not only were qualified, but also appointed to this purpose.

"Faith Comes by Hearing"

We acquire some knowledge by observation and much more by testimony from others. If our only means for learning were by our own observation, we would be severely limited in what we could know. Most of what we know about anything we learn from others. This is especially the case as to historical events. We can know nothing about the life, death, and resurrection of Jesus except by the testimony in Scripture. A line of rhetorical questions from Paul shows the logic in God's method.

> For "whoever calls on the name of the LORD shall be
> saved." How then shall they call on Him in whom they
> have not believed? And how shall they believe in Him
> of whom they have not heard? And how shall they
> hear without a preacher? And how shall they preach
> unless they are sent? (Romans 10:13-15a).

Faith is not a mysterious thing. A person believes when he hears (or reads) and is convinced that what he has been told is true. One cannot believe the gospel until it is communicated to him. "So then faith *comes* by hearing, and hearing by the word of God" (Romans 10:17). This is the process in every case of conversion described in the book of Acts. Peter explained, "God chose among us, that by my mouth the Gentiles should hear the word of the gospel and believe" (Acts 15:7). When the gospel was preached

> **"Nothing is so crucial to our eternal destiny
> as to whether we can be certain that
> Jesus died and rose again."**

at Corinth, "many of the Corinthians, hearing, believed and were baptized" (Acts 18:8). What was first delivered orally is available for all ages in the written word. The means by which people in Bible times were led to believe is the same thing that can produce faith in our hearts today. They heard the message and were convinced that the evidence was sufficient to prove it was true. Now the same testimony is written for us in the Bible. John stated the case that believing in Christ is on the basis of Scripture:

> *What is our single source of information about Jesus being the Christ, God's Son?*
>
> . . . .
>
> *What is God's plan for making people believers?*

... Jesus did many other signs in the presence of His disciples, which are not written in this book; but these are written that you may believe that Jesus is the Christ, the Son of God, and that believing you may have life in His name (John 20:30-31).

Credible Testimony (Luke 24:48; Acts 1:8)

Nothing is so crucial to our eternal destiny as to whether we can be certain that Jesus died and rose again. This is not settled by science. It is not a conclusion of philosophy. It cannot be by means of our own experience and observation. If it is to be known as fact, it must be established by evidence. The only evidence that exists is the testimony of the New Testament writers. We must either accept that what they tell us is true, or we must dismiss them as unreliable, as victims of duplicity, or as fraudulent conspirators. Either their record is true or it is false. There is no in between. Paul admitted that if Christ had not been raised, "[W]e are found false witnesses of God, because we have testified of God that He raised up Christ, whom He did not raise up — if in fact the dead do not rise" (1 Corinthians 15:15-16).

The same common-sense criteria that should be applied in determining the credibility of any testimony should be applied to the New Testament witnesses. Such is comparable to what would be considered in a court of law. It is as if saying, "Here are the witnesses, ready to be examined. Should they be believed?"

Were the New Testament writers **competent**? That is, were they men of sufficient intelligence to understand the issues and did they have the ability to give an accurate account of what had been seen and heard? The New Testament documents themselves demonstrate having been written by intelligent and capable men.

Did the witnesses have **personal knowledge** of the actual events? Did they know the persons and places involved, and were they present on the occasions described? Jesus affirmed the apostles' personal knowledge of Him. "And you also will bear witness, because you have been with Me from the beginning" (John 15:27). They were with Him during His ministry, saw Him die, and were with Him often after His resurrection (Acts 1:1ff, 21f; 10:39ff; 13:29). John was thorough in affirming his firsthand knowledge of "which we have heard, which we have seen with our eyes, which we have looked upon, and our hands have handled..." that which we have seen and heard we declare to you...." (1 John 1:1-2).

Did the apostolic witnesses have any **prior bias** that would have made them susceptible to a false impression of what they observed? In other words, were the apostles so predisposed to believe that Christ would arise that they would believe they saw Him even if they had not? No, instead their inclinations were the opposite. They had not understood His predictions. They were hopelessly bewildered by His death. To them, the first reports of His resurrection were nonsense (Luke 24:11). "Later He appeared to the eleven as they sat at the table; and He rebuked their unbelief and hardness of heart, because they did not believe those who had seen Him after He had risen" (Mark 16:14). It will be seen later that Paul's case is even stronger on this point because up to the time Jesus appeared to him, he was an enemy of Christ and the church.

Is there **harmony** among the witnesses? Rarely will two or more people observe an event in exactly the same way. When there are direct contradictions among any witnesses, some or all of their testimony cannot be accepted. On the other hand, two or three in agreement provides reasonable certainty (Deuteronomy 19:15; Matthew 18:16). The several New Testament writers are in perfect agreement as to Christ's having been seen after He arose. Differences in details or differences as to which events are reported are not contradictions — only evidence of no collusion among the writers.

Can we know the witnesses were **reliable** men? Can they be trusted to have been telling the truth? In human affairs, greater confidence is usually accorded statements made "under oath." A much higher affirmation validates the apostles. In the first place, nothing is known that would impugn their characters or motives. More to certainty, however, is that they were willing to die in support what they said. Some men may do extreme things in defense of something they know to be false, but hardly would any die for what they know is a lie. The New Testament witnesses made the supreme affirmation. They were willing to give up their lives for what they were convinced to be true. (See Acts 21:13; 2 Timothy 4:6-7; Revelation 12:11.)

What are five criteria for evaluating the credibility of a witness?

. . . .

To what degree do the apostolic witnesses meet each of these requirements?

Testimony of Holy Spirit (John 15:26)

In appointing them to be His witnesses, Jesus assured that their testimony would be in conjunction with the power of the Holy Spirit.

> And you are witnesses of these things. Behold, I send
> the Promise of My Father upon you; but tarry in the
> city of Jerusalem until you are endued with power
> from on high" (Luke 24:48-49).
>
> But you shall receive power when the Holy Spirit has
> come upon you; and you shall be witnesses to Me in
> Jerusalem, and in all Judea and Samaria, and to the
> end of the earth" (Acts 1:8).

Though the apostles met the criteria for creditable witnesses, their combined testimony could not have been perfect without divine assistance. Before His betrayal, during the upper room discourse, Jesus promised the apostles would be given a "Helper," the Holy Spirit. All Christians receive the Holy Spirit, but miraculous help (power) from the Holy Spirit was promised for the apostolic witnesses.

> But when the Helper comes, whom I shall send to you
> from the Father, the Spirit of truth who proceeds from
> the Father, He will testify of Me. And you also will
> bear witness, because you have been with Me from
> the beginning (John 15:26-27).
>
> And we are His witnesses to these things, and so also is
> the Holy Spirit whom God has given to those who obey
> Him (Acts 5:32).

In this context, "those who obey Him" refers to the apostles who were obeying Christ's command to be His witnesses. Their enemies had ordered them not to teach in Christ's name (v. 28).

But they were determined to obey Christ's command instead, the orders He had given to them in the Great Commission. The power that came with the Holy Spirit enabled them to give perfect testimony — inerrant and infallible. The Spirit working in them brought to their memory everything Jesus taught them (John 14:26) and guided them into all truth (John 16:13).

Further, the power that came with the Spirit provided miraculous signs, which verified their approval from the Lord. Not only were they qualified in every human way to be credible witnesses, but their testimony also was proven true by miraculous wonders. Their words being confirmed by "signs and wonders, with various miracles, and gifts of the Holy Spirit" (Hebrews 2:3-4a; see also Mark 16:20; Romans 15:19). We believe because of the Spirit-guided testimony recorded in the Scriptures.

The apostles "preached the gospel to you by the Holy Spirit sent from heaven" (1 Peter 1:12). At first this was in person; now it is provided in writing for all generations. Two of the Gospel writers were not apostles, but they also wrote under the guidance of the Holy Spirit. Mark, as a youthful member of the Jerusalem church, would have learned from Peter and the others. He also spent some time traveling with Barnabas and Paul and in later years would be named as one of Paul's "fellow laborers." Luke begins with affirming that his information came from those "which from the beginning were eyewitnesses, and ministers of the word" (Luke 1:2). In every case, the gospel story comes to us as indisputable testimony certified by the Holy Spirit.

By all reasonable standards, no facts as to any historical event could be more certainly verified. The decisive question comes down to whether the New Testament witnesses can be believed. Either the apostolic witnesses are credible or they are not. It is an enormous thing to charge witnesses with perjury. When credible witnesses say a certain thing happened, it behooves skeptics to prove otherwise. Honest, unprejudiced people, weighing the testimony, will believe the truth.

It is not within the scope of this study to prove the authenticity of the New Testament documents. There is abundant evidence that the New Testament books are what they claim to be, i.e., the writings of the men whose names they bear. The history they record is history from the times in which they lived. Except for those who are blinded by prejudice and unbelief, manuscript scholars have found no reason to doubt that we have the actual testimony of the apostolic witnesses.

Would the apostles' testimony have been sufficient without the help of the Holy Spirit?

. . . .

In what ways did the Holy Spirit assist their testimony?

. . . .

Why should we trust the New Testament writers who were not apostles?

CHAPTER EIGHT

Into Galilee, to the Mountain

AFTER ASSURING THE WOMEN THAT JESUS IS ALIVE, THE angel said, "[G]o tell His disciples — and Peter — that He is going before you into Galilee; there you will see Him, as He said to you" (Mark 16:7; Matthew 28:7). On their way, Jesus Himself met them and repeated the instruction: "Go and tell My brethren to go to Galilee, and there they will see Me" (Matthew 28:10). The specific promise about Galilee had been given in Gethsemane on the night of His betrayal (Matthew 26:32; Mark 14:28). The context was His predictions that He, the Shepherd, would be struck down and that "the sheep [His disciples] would be scattered." This promise was the only positive thing they heard in the garden that awful night. When these dreadful events were over, they would see Him again, and it would be in the familiar environs of Galilee.

In a few days, they would return to the familiar environment of Galilee. It is not known why they delayed leaving Judea for at least two Sundays. He had met with 10 apostles on the evening of the first Lord's Day and again the following Sunday with Thomas also being present. John records that the third meeting was with only seven apostles by the Sea of Tiberias/Galilee.

Breakfast by the Sea (John 21:1-23)

They had gone back to the place where they were first called to be fishers of men. Now, waiting and unsure what to do, Peter seemed ready to resume his previous occupation as a fisherman. The others went with him. The seven in the boat were Peter, Thomas, Nathanael, James, John, and two others (unnamed). They spent the night fishing, but caught nothing. Conversations through the night must have covered myriads of questions, their uncertainties, and their hopes.

As the rays of the sun were breaking behind them, they saw someone on the beach, but did not know it was Jesus. They were about a hundred yards out to sea when they heard Him call, "Children, do you have any food?" "No," they had fished through the night and caught nothing. He told them, "Cast the net on the right side of the boat, and you will find some." The immediate catch was too large to pull into the boat. This was more than fisherman's luck! John exclaimed to Peter, "It is the Lord!" Not waiting for the others, Peter hastily jumped into the water. The rest stayed with the boat and brought the net to the shore.

On the beach a breakfast of fish and bread was cooking on a charcoal fire. Jesus told them to bring some of the fish they had caught. It was a huge catch —153 large fish — remarkable in that so many could be in the net without it breaking. This called to memory a similar catch in the same waters (Luke 5:4-7). It was the same kind of miracle performed by the same Man. None had to ask because all knew it was the Lord. In fact, nothing is recorded as having been said by anyone until they had finished eating. This meal added one more proof that He was alive. Though here it is not said whether He actually ate, at the time of His first meeting with the group, He had eaten fish and honeycomb (Luke 24:41-43). Later, Peter would recall His eating and drinking with them as one of the many proofs of His resurrection (Acts 10:41).

> *What were the two previous times Jesus had met with apostles in a group?*
>
> . . . .
>
> *What are some comparisons or contrasts between the two occasions of miraculous catches?*

Restoration and Commission (John 21:15-23)

When they had finished breakfast, Jesus directly addressed Peter in a seemingly formal way by using his original name, "Simon, son of Jonah" (see also John 1:42; Matthew 16:18). This may suggest that Simon needed to be reminded that the name Peter (Cephas, a rock) had been given to him when he had shown great firmness of faith by confessing Christ as the Son of God. His conscience would know that his denials on the night of Christ's betrayal raised questions as to whether he deserved the nickname. Earlier that betrayal night, he had boasted, "Even if all are made to stumble because of You, I will never be made to stumble" (Matthew 26:33; Mark 14:29). But Jesus warned that three times he would deny his Lord before the night was over (Matthew 26:33-35; Mark 14:30).

The circumstances of those denials were less threatening than might have been imagined. Two girls and a bystander had recognized him. As for the third time he disavowed knowing his Lord, he saw Jesus turn to look at him. Peter's remorse was immediate and bitter (Matthew 26:69-75; Luke 22:54-62; John 18:15-18, 25-27). We need not doubt that Peter had genuinely repented, nor whether he still felt a great burden of conscience. Peter had already seen Jesus privately on the first Lord's Day, but we are not told of anything said. As far as we can know, therefore, the issue of his denials was still hanging unresolved. Thus, Jesus' three questions as to Peter's loyalty juxtapose his three denials. It is interesting, perhaps on purpose, that they were here by the same kind of fire, a charcoal fire, by which Peter was standing in the high priest's courtyard.

> So when they had eaten breakfast, Jesus said to Simon Peter, "Simon, son of Jonah, do you love Me more than these?"He said to Him, "Yes, Lord; You know that I love You." He said to him, "Feed My lambs." He said to him again a second time, "Simon, son of Jonah, do you love Me?" He said to Him, "Yes, Lord; You know that I love You." He said to him, "Tend My sheep." He said to him the third time, "Simon, son of Jonah, do you love Me?" Peter was grieved because He said to him the third time, "Do you love Me?" And he said to Him, "Lord, You know all things; You know that I love You." Jesus said to him, "Feed My sheep" (John 21:15-17).

This is about rehabilitation. This deeply fallen follower can be restored to a place of leadership. He who knows our hearts better than we know ourselves did not ask these questions for His own assurance, but to restore Peter's confidence in himself. Now, his profession of love is not the boast of the betrayal night, but with the humility of a restored penitent.

As simple as this exchange is, there has been much speculation over the significance of the words used. First, it is noticed that "more than these" could mean "these things," referring to the boat, net, fish (i.e., his fisherman profession), in which case the issue would be whether he loved Christ enough to leave that profession and devote his life to spiritual service. On the other hand, the question might have been "more than these other disciples." His earlier boast had allowed for their disloyalty, but not for his own. Could he still make such a claim? His contrition avoided even reference at all to the others. He simply said, "Yes, Lord; You know that I love You."

Attention also should be given to the different Greek words translated love. In the first two questions, Jesus used the verb *agapaoo*, which indicates unselfish devotion. Possibly, Peter chose a different word out of modesty. The term he used for love (*phileoo*) relates more to natural affection, which comes from admiration and relationship. However, we need not suppose that Peter chose a different word to excuse himself or to shrink from the demands of full devotion love (*agape*). The words have too much overlap of meaning to suppose there is any conflict. In the third question, Jesus Himself switches to *phileoo*, which shows His acceptance of Peter's word choice. What mattered was that Peter must understand the necessity of love and loyalty needed for the commission Jesus was giving him.

The wording of Peter's commission was to be a "shepherd" for the "lambs" and "sheep," Those who were followers of Christ would need Peter's attention and care. If a distinction was intended by the use of different words for the flock, probably it is only to suggest that some are more mature than others. Likewise, "Feed My lambs" and "Tend My sheep" use different imperatives to comprehend everything needed for their spiritual care: feed, tending, protection.

Shepherding is a frequent scriptural metaphor for spiritual leadership (1 Peter 5:1-4). This responsibility assigned to Peter need not suggest he was given a different or higher office than assigned to the other apostles. It seems more likely that he is given this special attention because of his vocal denials. Other texts show that all the apostles received the same commission and authority.

Then followed a sobering prediction of what would be in the future for Simon Peter. He had in his youth and vigor chosen as a free man to follow Jesus. He would live to be an old man, but death would come by the hands of others. His love for Christ would eventually lead to martyrdom. Nevertheless, Jesus expects, "Follow Me."

The conversation ends with Peter shifting attention to John as to what would be in his future. Jesus answered, "If I will that he remain till I come, what is that to you? You follow Me" (John 21:22).

How were Peter's denials inconsistent with the name Jesus had given him?

. . . .

What seems to be the reason for Peter being questioned three times?

. . . .

What are the different contexts of the two times Jesus told Peter to follow Him?

At the Appointed Mountain (Matthew 28:16-20)

All Christ's appearances except one were surprises. They occurred without expectation. This meeting with the 11 was at an appointed place on a mountain in Galilee. Jesus had promised such a meeting, and it had been reaffirmed by the angels and Jesus Himself (Matthew 26:32; 28:7, 10). Whether others than the 11 were present is not revealed. There had been other times when He addressed the apostles though others were close by. It is likely Justus and Matthias were present (Acts 1:22), as well as the women who had been told of the meeting. Some scholars think this was the occasion when 500 saw Him. Regardless, Matthew specifically names the 11, which indicates His instructions as particularly pertaining to them. "When they saw Him, they worshiped Him; but some doubted." How Thomas's doubts had been overcome

> "Shepherding is a frequent scriptural metaphor for spiritual leadership... This responsibility assigned to Peter need not suggest he was given a different or higher office than assigned to the other apostles."

has already been told. Matthew does not mean there was ongoing doubt, only that they had been unwilling to believe until they saw for themselves.

Though the account of this meeting is brief, it is of special significance because it involves what is often called the Great Commission. It is called "great" in contrast to a "limited" commission, which had been given earlier (Matthew 10:5-15). At that time, they had been sent only to the "lost sheep of the house of Israel." Now the message was for all the world, Gentiles as well as Jews. It may also properly be called the "Apostolic Commission." Every Christian and the church in every age should be involved in spreading the gospel, but it would be specifically the apostles, who would authoritatively inaugurate the Christian system. The opening statement of Acts refers to it as "commandments to the apostles." They would lay the foundation (Ephesians 2:20). No one would ever be appointed to revise or amend the original message (1 Corinthians 3:11; 2 John 9). The mission of the church from the beginning has been to abide by and preach the same (2 Timothy 2:2).

In the closed room meeting on the evening of the first Lord's Day, Jesus had spoken of their mission. "Peace to you! As the Father has sent Me, I also send you" (John 20:21). Now, in this mountain setting, He gives more specific instructions as to the purpose for which He would send them.

> And Jesus came and spoke to them, saying, "All authority has been given to Me in heaven and on earth. Go therefore and make disciples of all the nations, baptizing them in the name of the Father and of the Son and of the Holy Spirit, teaching them to observe all things that I have commanded you; and lo, I am with you always, even to the end of the age" (Matthew 28:18-20).

It would not be possible for people of all nations to be Christ's disciples without being taught His commandments. By being taught they could become disciples by being baptized in the name of the Father, Son, and Holy Spirit. All was by the authority of Christ through the administration of His apostles.

There seems to be a unique significance in the promise to be with them to the end of the world. They would not, of course, continue in the world to the end, but the authority of the "apostles' doctrine" continues in place. All Christians have the assurance of the Lord's constant presence. "For He Himself has said, 'I will never leave you nor forsake you'" (Hebrews 13:5).

What may be the reason Matthew mentions only the 11 being at this meeting?

. . . .

At what earlier meeting had Jesus spoken of sending them?

> *Would it be possible for people to become disciples without being taught?*
>
> . . . .
>
> *At what point does a taught person actually become a disciple?*

However, in the way the promise is here connected with the Apostolic Commission, it seems to indicate that their place as Christ's spokesmen would stay in place until the end of the world. The practical significance of this for today is that Christian faith and practice should always be consistent with the pattern set by the apostles.

In Mark and Luke (Mark 16:15-18; Luke 24:44-49)

Jesus had met with the apostles at various times over the 40 days before His ascension, which provided many occasions for the Commission commandment to be repeated. It is not clear whether Mark's record of the commission was quoted from this mountain meeting or from another occasion, but they are obviously connected.

> "Go into all the world and preach the gospel to every creature. He who believes and is baptized will be saved; but he who does not believe will be condemned. And these signs will follow those who believe: In My name they will cast out demons; they will speak with new tongues; they will take up serpents; and if they drink anything deadly, it will by no means hurt them; they will lay hands on the sick, and they will recover."
> ...And they went out and preached everywhere, the Lord working with them and confirming the word through the accompanying signs (Mark 16:15-18, 20).

Luke's narrative also provides a record of the Apostolic Commission. Just as with Mark, we cannot be certain as to when Jesus spoke the words quoted in Luke. Some scholars have thought Luke was quoting from a final meeting back in Jerusalem. Regardless, it cannot be doubted that what is recorded by all four was under the guidance of the Holy Spirit and essential for our understanding.

> Then He said to them, "Thus it is written, and thus it was necessary for the Christ to suffer and to rise from the dead the third day, and that repentance and remission of sins should be preached in His name to all nations, beginning at Jerusalem. And you are witnesses of these things. Behold, I send the Promise of My Father upon you; but tarry in the city of Jerusalem until you are endued with power from on high" (Luke 24:46-49).

Both Mark and Luke emphasize that the miraculous signs that would accompany the apostles in this mission. Such power was promised to the apostles and not to all believers. They were the appointed witnesses (Acts 1:8; Hebrews 2:3-4). Though some others in the early church were given miraculous gifts, it was always in connection with the laying on of the apostles' hands (Acts 8:15-18).

The history of how the apostles carried out their mission is the purpose of the book of Acts. Though the wording of the Great Commission is not difficult to understand, the conversion stories in Acts give perfect demonstrations of what Jesus intended for the apostles to do and to teach.

(The arrangement of the following review questions is intended to reemphasize how the four accounts overlap and blend together.)

Which of the four statements of the Apostolic Commission specifically mentions the following?

- *The beginning would be in Jerusalem?*

- *Christ has absolute authority?*

- *The apostles were Christ's "witnesses"?*

- *As the Father had sent Jesus, so they (apostles) were being sent?*

- *The fundamental facts to be preached were Christ's passion and resurrection?*

- *Making disciples involved baptizing those who were taught?*

- *They were to preach and require repentance?*

- *They would have power to confirm their message by miracles?*

- *The apostles were delegated to teach everything Jesus commanded?*

- *Salvation is for one who believes and is baptized?*

- *The apostles' commission was till the end of the age?*

Above 500 at Once (1 Corinthians 15:6)

In Paul's "Resurrection Chapter," he gives a partial list of eyewitnesses. Included is an otherwise unknown reference to 500. "After that He was seen by over five hundred brethren at once, of whom the greater part remain to the present, but some have fallen asleep." At the time this was stated, Paul implied that this was an easily verified event because most were still alive. It could hardly be expected that so large a group would have been deceived as to what they saw or that so many would have conspired in such a falsehood and continue to maintain it as long as they lived.

Likely this was somewhere in Galilee where there were larger numbers of Jesus' followers. In Jerusalem after Christ's ascension, there had been at least 120 men and women, but in Galilee, where most of His miracles and teaching had been done, there would be many more. For so many to have gathered at one time suggests prior knowledge of the appointment. Though particular attention was given to His appointment with the apostles, news certainly would have spread abroad. His Galilean followers would have heard reports that He was alive and would have embraced any opportunity to see Him.

Why would we think Christ's appearance to 500 at once was likely in Galilee and that the event was well-known in the early years of the church?

. . . .

What was Paul's reason for stating most of the 500 were still alive?

James (1 Corinthians 15:7)

We know Paul's naming of eyewitnesses is not a complete list, but those included are in chronological order. After reference to the otherwise unknown 500 and before the last meeting with the apostles, we are told that Christ was seen by James. Which James was this? It was not the brother of John, who early in the church's history was murdered by Herod (Acts 12:1-2). This predated the writing of 1 Corinthians. Another prominent James, the son of Alpheus, was also one of the apostles. In another of Paul's letters, particular attention is given to the James who was Jesus' half-brother. He was prominent in the Jerusalem church and author of one, eponymous New Testament book (Galatians 1:19; 2:9). Early in Jesus' ministry, His brothers had not believed in Him, but after the ascension, they were with other believers in Jerusalem (John 7:5; Acts 1:13-14). Many Bible students think this is the James whom Paul mentioned as having seen Jesus.

As to what was the place or occasion of Jesus' meeting with James, we are not told. All other appearances were in either Judea or Galilee. Paul's matter-of-fact reference to this James assumes his readers would know about him. It is not important for us to know details, only to be assured that he was one of the many witnesses.

> *Inasmuch as we cannot certainly identify this James, how is Paul's reference to him important?*

CHAPTER NINE

He Was Taken Up

JESUS APPEARED TO HIS FOLLOWERS AT VARIOUS TIMES AND places for 40 days. We are not told the actual number of times, but we know the occasions were used not only to prove Himself alive, but also to instruct His apostles about His coming kingdom. Only 12 specific meetings are named, and six of these had been on the first two Sundays in or near Jerusalem. After that He met with His followers at places in Galilee and finally with just the Twelve back in Judea and at the Mount of Olives.

The emphasis on the apostles' mission at the end of Luke is continued as Acts begins. Their work could not be successful without Divine assistance. Thus, Jesus instructed that they were to wait in Jerusalem until they received the promised baptism of the Holy Spirit. "John truly baptized with water, but you shall be baptized with the Holy Spirit not many days from now" (Acts 1:5). John the Baptist had foretold that Christ would baptize with the Spirit, but did not indicate to whom it would be given. Jesus applied the promise specifically to the apostles.

Though Jesus had taught them much about the coming kingdom, at the time of this meeting they still seemed unable to understand its spiritual nature. They asked, "Lord, will You at this time restore the kingdom to Israel?" (v. 6). The short answer was that it was not for them to know the time, which was in God's hands. They had been assured, however, that when the kingdom came, it would come with power.

> But you will receive power when the Holy Spirit comes on you; and you will be my witnesses in Jerusalem, and in all Judea and Samaria, and to the ends of the earth. (Acts 1:8, ESV).

The kingdom would come with power, and the power would come with the baptism of the Holy Spirit. "Power" meant being guided into "all truth." It also meant supernatural validation of their testimony (John 16:13; Mark 16:17-18). This would occur in only a few days. The day of the coming of the Holy Spirit upon the apostles would be the day that would be the beginning of the promised kingdom of heaven on earth. That day would be on the day of Pentecost, some 10 days later.

How would the baptism of the Holy Spirit relate to the coming of the kingdom?

. . . .

Did Jesus indicate a time and place for the beginning of their mission?

. . . .

When the Spirit came, what kind of power would the apostles receive?

The Ascension (Mark 16:19; Luke 24:50-53; Acts 1:9-12)

On the day of His ascension, Jesus led them out from Jerusalem to the Mount of Olives at Bethany and with uplifted hands blessed them. Then, He was taken up into the sky. During His ministry on earth, He had repeatedly emphasized that He would return to heaven. "I came forth from the Father and have come into the world. Again, I leave the world and go to the Father" (John 16:28). For 40 days, He had shown infallible evidence that after having been killed and buried, He is now alive. The ascension completes the story of God sending His Son into the world. Not only did He come back to life, He is even now and always will be the living Lord. From heaven, Jesus assures, "I am He who lives, and was dead, and behold, I am alive forevermore." (Revelation 1:18).

The ascension also answers the question of what happened to the body of Jesus. The issue of the empty grave cannot be forgotten. Certainly, over the centuries many bodies have disappeared, never to be found. In the case of Christ, however, the circumstances allow no trivial explanation. Witnesses watched the burial. Professional soldiers guarded the tomb. It was only a few hours between the burial Friday evening and the body's disappearance on Sunday morning. Both friends and enemies knew the exact location and confirmed that the tomb was vacant. Enemies were so perplexed that they concocted a ridiculous explanation. His friends, after initial dismay over the empty grave, had become convinced that He is alive.

Thus, the question has become a theoretical playground for skeptics. The Jews said His body was stolen, but no corpse was ever found. The swoon theory supposed He had not been really dead when buried. Yet, even if so, eventually He would have died. Where is the body? Numerous have been the artifacts claimed to have been associated with Jesus. The one thing never found, however, any evidence of His last remains.

Into the Clouds

"While they watched, He was taken up, and a cloud received Him out of their sight" (Acts 1:9). As they watched Him ascend, the clouds first were a backdrop to frame their vision and afterward a veil to block their view. Out of their sight, He passed into Heaven itself to take His place at the right hand of God. This is not to say that heaven is just on the other side of clouds, only that they were not permitted to see Him take on His glorious form, nor to see Him ushered into the realm of God's eternal glory. Though their view was of the visible universe, Jesus "ascended far above all the heavens," that is, beyond this universe into the eternal heaven.

On the various occasions when He had appeared to the disciples, He presented Himself in ways fitted to human experience. Such was necessary to impress that this was the body that had died. He could be touched. His wounds were shown. He walked and talked. He ate food. This was "flesh and bones," not a ghost (Luke 24:39). All of this was to satisfy questions as to whether a dead corpse really had come back to life. It is true, of course, that at the same time He possessed extraordinary powers not consistent with a fleshly body, but such in no way mitigates the fact that it was the body of Jesus they saw, and it was His body (not a ghost/spirit) they watched ascend.

It is not to be missed, therefore, that it was really He they saw taken up. The One ascending was the very One who had just lifted His arms in blessing them. The one who ascended was the One who had descended, i.e., "the Son of man." John 3:13 says, "No one has ascended to heaven but He who came down from heaven, that is, the Son of Man who is in heaven." The same point is in Ephesians 4:10: "He who descended is also the One who ascended far above all the heavens..." Their fixed gaze had stayed on the place they last could see Him until angels appeared and said, "Men of Galilee, why do you stand gazing up into heaven? This same Jesus, who was taken up from you into heaven, will so come in like manner as you saw Him go into heaven." (See also 1 Thessalonians 1:10; 4:16-17; Revelation 1:7; 2 Thessalonians 1:7-10).

He was taken up in His earthly body and received into heaven in "His glorious body" (Philippians 3:21). This does not mean He ceased to be "the man" they saw taken up. Paul spoke of our one mediator between God and man as "the man Christ Jesus" (1 Timothy 2:5). He is the same man, only now He has a body fitted for glory. Nothing in our world's comparisons makes it possible to picture a glorified body. John wrote that "it has not yet been revealed what we shall be, but we know that when He is revealed, we shall be like Him, for we shall see Him as He is" (1 John 3:2).

In Paul's discussion of our own bodies in the resurrection, he explains that "flesh and blood cannot inherit the kingdom of God," but that God will provide a body, a "spiritual body (1 Corinthians 15:44). It is not to be understood that "spiritual" implies merely a spirit. The spirit is one thing, the body another. When Christ's spirit left His body, His body was dead. In His resurrection, His Spirit returned, and His now ever-alive body passed beyond the clouds and took on immortality, but He is still "the man Christ Jesus." The promise for us is, "And as we have borne the image of the man of dust, we shall also bear the image of the heavenly Man" (1 Corinthians 15:35-50). The same assurance is in Philippians 3, which promises that Christ "will transform our lowly body that it may be conformed to His glorious body, according to the working by which He is able even to subdue all things to Himself" (v. 21).

Was the ascension part of God's original plan?

. . . .

In what ways had Jesus proven to the disciples that His body was real?

. . . .

When will we be able to see Him as He is now?

His Coronation (Mark 16:19; Hebrews 1:3-12; Ephesians 1:19-23; 1 Peter 3:22)

Mark's account of the ascension says, "He was received up into heaven, and sat down at the right hand of God" (Mark 16:19). Paul affirms that God "seated Him at His right hand in the heavenly places, far above all principality and power and might and dominion, and every name that is named, not only in this age but also in that which is to come" (Ephesians 1:20-21). Peter wrote that Christ "has gone into heaven and is at the right hand of God, angels and authorities and powers having been made subject to Him" (1 Peter 3:22).

The remarkable 24th Psalm gives a choral refrain extolling His reception as He comes to the throne room of God.

> Lift up your heads, O you gates! And be lifted up, you everlasting doors! And the King of glory shall come in. Who is this King of glory? The Lord strong and mighty, The Lord mighty in battle. Lift up your heads, O you gates! Lift up, you everlasting doors! And the King of glory shall come in. Who is this King of glory? The Lord of hosts, He is the King of glory (Psalm 24:7-10).

Consider, too, the vision shown to John, the wonderful exultation of our Redeemer being sung by myriad angels:

> Then I looked, and I heard the voice of many angels around the throne, the living creatures, and the elders; and the number of them was ten thousand times ten thousand, and thousands of thousands, saying with a loud voice: "Worthy is the Lamb who was slain to receive power and riches and wisdom, And strength

and honor and glory and blessing!" And every
creature which is in heaven and on the earth and
under the earth and such as are in the sea, and all
that are in them, I heard saying: "Blessing and honor
and glory and power be to Him who sits on the throne,
And to the Lamb, forever and ever!" Then the four
living creatures said, "Amen!" And the twenty-four
elders fell down and worshiped Him who lives forever
and ever (Revelation 5:11-14).

In their last interview, the disciples had asked about the coming of the kingdom. Jesus' answer was that it was in God's hands. There could be no kingdom until the King was crowned. Something had to take place in heaven before the kingdom could be established on earth. He ascended into the clouds and was gone from their view. They could not see His reception in glory. However, a prophetic vision described by Daniel tells what happened on the other side of those clouds.

I was watching in the night visions, And behold, One
like the Son of Man, Coming with the clouds of
heaven! He came to the Ancient of Days, And they
brought Him near before Him. Then to Him was given
dominion and glory and a kingdom, That all peoples,
nations, and languages should serve Him. His dominion
is an everlasting dominion, Which shall not pass
away, And His kingdom the one Which shall not be
destroyed (Daniel 7:13-14).

Earlier in Daniel, it had been prophesied that "the God of heaven will set up a kingdom which shall never be destroyed"

(Daniel 2:44). This is the kingdom established when Jesus ascended and took His place at the right hand of God (Mark 16:19). The kingdom of heaven was established on earth when the King was crowned in heaven.

> "There could be no kingdom until the King was crowned."

Jesus was born to be King. He was incarnated into flesh that He might die. He died that He might be raised. He was raised that He might ascend. He ascended that He might be crowned. He was crowned to be "King of kings and Lord of lords." This took place in heaven. It is not, and never will be, an earthly, political kingdom. It is "not of this world" (John 18:36). Rather, it is a spiritual kingdom, the rule of Christ in the hearts and lives of believers. The earthly manifestation of the kingdom of heaven on earth is the church. The King of the kingdom is the Head of the church (Ephesians 1:20-22).

In what way does Daniel's vision compare to the ascension as described in Acts 1?

Why was it necessary for Him to ascend before the kingdom could be established?

How does His being King over the kingdom correspond with His being Head of the church?

CHAPTER TEN

They Taught the People and Preached

THE FIRST OFFICIAL PERSECUTION AGAINST THE APOSTLES'
work came from the Sadducees, a sect of the Jews who did not
believe in the possibility of any resurrection, much less that of
Jesus. "Now as they spoke to the people, the priests, the captain
of the temple, and the Sadducees came upon them, being greatly
disturbed that they taught the people and preached in Jesus the
resurrection from the dead" (Acts 4:1-2). The gospel could not be
preached without emphasis on Jesus' coming back from death. The
story of the resurrection continues with the spread of this message
into all the world.

Pentecost (Acts 2:1-13)

Thousands who had come from many nations had gathered in
Jerusalem for the annual feast of Pentecost. It had been 50 days
since the crucifixion and 10 days since Jesus had ascended to

heaven. As Jesus had instructed, the apostles had been continually in the temple waiting for the promise of the Spirit. They had a story to tell, but waited for authority and power to tell it. Suddenly on that Sunday morning, noise like a violent wind came from above and what appeared as flames of fire sat on each of the 12. This unique phenomenon, never known before or since, accompanied their being baptized of the Holy Spirit, by which they were "endued with power from on high" (Luke 24:49). Their minds and lips immediately came under the influence of the Spirit, and they began to declare the wonderful works of God. The miracle was evident in that they were speaking in the languages of many nations.

As news of this marvel spread, crowds gathered in confusion. "What does this mean?" Though people were perplexed by what they saw and heard, we are not to assume the apostles were speaking in a frantic and disorderly way. This was not an ecstatic frenzy. Their speech was deliberate and calm, as they intelligibly declared great things of God. Miraculously, these simple Galileans had become fluent in every vernacular present. Some irreverent skeptics mocked, but thousands perceived this had to have come from God and wanted to hear what the apostles had to say.

Several factors made this astonished crowd a receptive audience. They were religious people who accepted the Scriptures as the inspired word of God. The Bible describes them as "devout men." They believed and held to the Jewish hope of the promised Messiah. They had come to Jerusalem from many places, but news of recent events was on the public mind. The great Teacher from Nazareth had been crucified. Stories were being circulated about the disappearance of His body. Many had heard rumors of His resurrection. The implausibility of the guards' report was obvious. Doubtless, stories had also circulated about Judas, a known disciple of Jesus, how he had killed himself and the grotesque condition in which his body had been found (Matthew 27:3-5; Acts 1:18-19). These were troubling times, and the people wanted explanations.

Why were the apostles still together in Jerusalem?

. . . .

Who experienced the baptism of the Holy Spirit?

. . . .

What are some things that must have been on the public mind in Jerusalem?

. . . .

What compelled most of the crowd to give attention to the apostles?

Now, the obvious miracle miraculous tongues and the eloquence of the message gave credibility to the men who were speaking. The first sermon in the Christian age would be preached to people who already believed in God, who respected the authority of Scripture and who, as Jews, had expectations of the coming of the Messianic kingdom. "So they were all amazed and perplexed, saying to one another, 'Whatever could this mean?'" (Acts 2:12).

Miracle Explained (Acts 2:14-21)

Each of the apostles was involved, but it is Peter's words that are recorded. He began by citing a prophecy from Joel. Over eight centuries before, that prophet had foreseen the outpouring of the Spirit at the inauguration of a new age (Joel 2:28-30). Peter said, "This is that..." The miracle showed that the prophecy was beginning to be fulfilled. On that day (Pentecost) the "last days" had begun. A new dispensation, a new system, was being ushered into place. It was called the "last days" because this new age would continue till the end of the world. (See also Hebrew 1:2.) Jesus had said that the preaching of repentance and remission of sins "in His name" would begin at Jerusalem (Luke 24:47). This is what was happening. For the first time, the full gospel of the death, burial, and resurrection of Christ would be openly preached, and for the first time, salvation was to be offered through His name. Years later, Peter would refer to the events of that Pentecost as "the beginning." It was the beginning of the Christian age, the beginning of preaching the full gospel, the beginning of the kingdom/church.

The purpose of the immediate miracle of tongues was to prove divine certification of the speakers (apostles). Just as "miracles, wonders and signs," had validated Jesus' ministry, so supernatural phenomena provided through the apostles would confirm that they, too, had a message from God. (See also Hebrews 2:3-4.)

During the early history of the church, as the gospel message spread, such signs would continue with the apostles and certain of their coworkers. Such were temporary necessities that would cease when the perfect/complete revelation of Scripture was in place (1 Corinthians 13:8-13). The Holy Spirit had come upon the apostles with the promised enabling power. The miracle itself, as well as the cited prophecy, was enough to hold the crowd's attention.

> "Then came the boldest and most consequential declaration in all human history. This man, Jesus of Nazareth, had been raised up from death."

The miraculous gifts, which would be abundant in the beginning, were important and interesting, but it was not intended that they should be the identifying

According to Joel, the coming of the Holy Spirit indicated the beginning of what?

. . . .

Did all the things named by Joel occur on Pentecost?

. . . .

What was the purpose of miraculous signs during the apostolic age?

. . . .

In what ways does Joel's prophecy compare to what Jesus said would begin in Jerusalem?

feature of the new age. Instead, God's promise through Joel was, "And it shall come to pass that whoever calls on the name of the Lord shall be saved" (Acts 2:21, Joel 2:32). The prophecy explained the involvement of the Holy Spirit, but Peter immediately moves attention away from that to its emphasis on Jesus. Jesus had said concerning the Holy Spirit, "He will glorify Me, for He will take of what is Mine and declare it to you" (John 16:13-14). In this new age, this new order in the redemptive plan of God, everything about salvation would be centered on the name of Jesus Christ. "Repentance and remission of sins" would now be preached in His name to all nations.

Preaching Jesus (Acts 2:22-36)

Clearly, the point most urgent in Peter's sermon was not miraculous gifts, as impressive as they might be, but rather on the promise of salvation in the name of the Lord Jesus. Peter does not dwell long on the background story of Jesus. The multitude knew of His miracles, wonders, and signs, all of which attested to God's working through Him. They already knew that by the instigation of their own nation the heathen Romans had crucified Him. Regardless of whether any of them ever had direct involvement with Jesus, His murder was a scandal on the national conscience. Yet Peter assured that all had taken place as foreseen by God and according to the divine purpose. It remained for them to hear the rest of the story.

Then came the boldest and most consequential declaration in all human history. This man, Jesus of Nazareth, had been raised up from death. He had been set free from "the pains of death, because it was not possible that He should be held by it" (v. 24). The irreversible had been reversed. The collective wisdom of mankind held that chains of death cannot be broken, but God had broken them. Indeed, this was the very thing the Scriptures had promised.

> For David says concerning Him: "I have set the LORD always before me; Because He is at my right hand I shall not be moved. Therefore my heart is glad, and my glory rejoices; My flesh also will rest in hope. For You will not leave my soul in Sheol, Nor will You allow Your Holy One to see corruption. You will show me the path of life; In Your presence is fullness of joy; At Your right hand are pleasures forevermore" (Psalm 16:8-11).

Under God's presence and care, David was confident his flesh (his dead body) would not be laid to rest without hope. His soul would not be left in the unseen sphere of disembodied spirits (Hades). Neither would God allow his flesh to see corruption (decay). That David anticipated a resurrection cannot be missed. In fact, however, this had not been realized for David himself. As Peter reminded them, David had been dead for a long time.

His body was interred in a well-known sepulcher there in Jerusalem. Either David was mistaken, else he was referring to someone other than himself. The answer came from another well-known thread of Scripture:

> "Therefore, [David] being a prophet, and knowing that God had sworn with an oath to him that of the fruit of his body, according to the flesh, He would raise up the Christ to sit on his throne, he, foreseeing this, spoke concerning the resurrection of the Christ, that His soul was not left in Hades, nor did His flesh see corruption" (Acts 2:30-31).

In Luke's account of the Great Commission, what was to be preached in the name of the Lord?

. . . .

Was the crowd already aware of the life and death of Jesus?

. . . .

Why would David have used first-person references when pointing to the coming Messiah?

That the Messiah (Christ) would be of the seed of David was clearly prophesied and beyond dispute in the Jewish mind. David habitually had spoken in the first person because he saw the coming Messiah (Christ), who would be descended from him, as an extension of himself.

Certified Witnesses (Acts 2:32-36)

The life, ministry, and death of Jesus was common knowledge. Had they wondered how so great a man could have come to so ignoble an end? In fact, His death actually was in the predetermined purposes of God, and it was never intended or possible that death could hold Him permanently. Now Peter declares the one glorious fact that brought it all together: "This Jesus God has raised up, of which we are all witnesses" (v. 32).

This was not a mere interpretation, though it did explain the meaning of Scriptures. Neither was it theological speculation. It was a fact, proofs of which the apostles could testify they themselves had seen. How much they expanded on the evidence is not recorded, but the text explains, "And with many other words he testified and exhorted... " (v. 40). Their testimony could have included any or all of the occasions when they had seen, heard, and touched the living Christ.

Though not stated in the text, the next logical question would be, *If Jesus had been dead and buried, and if indeed He was then seen alive, where is He now?* Questions about His body being missing had circulated, aided by the dubious rumor about the tomb guards. If He resurrected and is alive, where is He now? What ultimately happened to Him? The promise to David was that Christ would be raised up (resurrected) "to sit on his [David's] throne" (v. 30).

> "Therefore being exalted to the right hand of God, and having received from the Father the promise of the Holy Spirit, He poured out this which you now see and hear" (v. 33).

The necessary inference from the prophecy ("therefore") is that the One "raised up" must be on David's throne at the right hand of God. The apostles saw Him disappear into the sky, but they could not testify as witnesses to His enthronement.

That the promise was certainly fulfilled was evident in the baptism of the Holy Spirit, the evidence of which they were seeing and hearing. It could only be from Christ's place in heaven that He could have manifested such power. That a miracle was happening before them could hardly be denied. Nor could they doubt the involvement of these 12 men. The Holy Spirit certified their credibility. "Therefore let all the house of Israel know assuredly that God has made this Jesus, whom you crucified, both Lord and Christ" (v. 36).

Then, as further proof that Messiah's throne is in heaven, Peter cites another of David's prophecies, "The LORD said to my Lord, 'Sit at My right hand, Till I make Your enemies Your footstool'" (Psalm 110:1). Peter's point was that for Him to be at God's right hand in heaven, He must have ascended into heaven. It was not David who had been raised from the grave, and it was not David who had ascended.

Why is Christ's throne in heaven referred to as David's throne?

. . . .

How did the miracle wrought by the Holy Spirit prove that Jesus was in heaven?

. . . .

How does Psalm 110 relate to the other prophecies cited from David?

. . . .

What had been seen and heard by the crowd that supported the credibility of these witnesses?

"When They Heard This" (Acts 2:26-47)

Jesus had emphasized preaching as the means by which people could be made believers. The apostles preached the gospel to this great crowd in Jerusalem. Faith develops in human hearts when people hear and accept the truth that is preached (Romans 10:17.) The process by which so many were converted on that day is stated quite clearly. Peter had urged them to believe, i.e., "know assuredly" (be fully convinced). "Now when they heard this, they were cut to the heart, and said to Peter and the rest of the apostles, 'Men and brethren, what shall we do?'" (v. 37).

It should be remembered that in the beginning of his speech, Peter's quotation from the prophet Joel promised salvation by calling on the name of the Lord. To call on the Lord's name is not to be understood as simply saying His name (Luke 6:46). Neither is it limited to calling on Him in prayer. Being convinced that the message is true — they believed what they heard — they asked what to do. That is, they asked how to call on the name of the Lord.

> Then Peter said to them, "Repent, and let every one of you be baptized in the name of Jesus Christ for the remission of sins; and you shall receive the gift of the Holy Spirit"...Then those who gladly received his word were baptized; and that day about three thousand souls were added to them (vv. 38, 41).

That repenting and being baptized is "in the name of Jesus Christ" shows that such obedience is action that is necessary to "call on" (i.e., to appeal to) Jesus Christ for remission of sins. (This emphasis on Christ's name in connection with baptism will be found in other conversion stories, e. g., Acts 8:16; 10:48; 19:5; 22:16; 1 Corinthians 6:11.).

Here are demonstrated all the elements of the Great Commission. It was at the right beginning place — Jerusalem.

The baptism of the Holy Spirit came on the apostles in fulfillment of prophecy. The apostles were certified as Christ's agents to declare whose sins were to be remitted. The gospel being preached, people believed, repented and were baptized in Christ's name. The apostles continued to instruct them to observe Christ's commandments. This was the first day of the new Christian age, the inauguration of Christ's kingdom, the beginning of Christ's church. From that day till now, saved people are members of Christ's church.

The history of the Book of Acts tells how the story of Jesus was taken throughout the Roman Empire and to faraway places, but the message never changed. Soon there was opposition by unbelievers and even murderous persecution. Still, Christians held on. They knew the gospel is true, that hope is real, because "Christ died for our sins... and that He was buried, and that He rose again the third day."

What method is used by God to convince people to believe?

. . . .

What does it mean to call on the name of Christ and how is this demonstrated in Acts 2?

. . . .

Is there any part of the Great Commission that does not fit the narrative of Acts 2?

CHAPTER ELEVEN

Born Out of Due Time

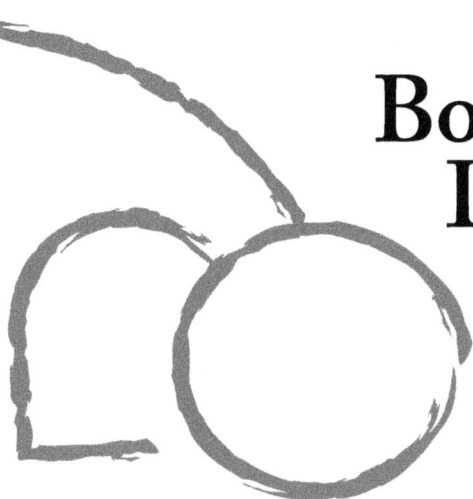

IN DEFENDING HIS APOSTLESHIP, PAUL DEMANDED, "AM I not an apostle? Am I not free? Have I not seen Jesus Christ our Lord?" (1 Corinthians 9:1). Rhetorical questions assume facts generally known. One qualification for being an apostle was to have been an eyewitness of the risen and living Christ (Acts 1:22). The story of how Paul, also known as Saul, became one of Christ's special witnesses, an apostle, is told three times in the history of Acts. Luke gives it as it fits in the chronological narrative (Acts 9). Paul told it in his own words to a large mob in Jerusalem (Acts 22) and again in a court hearing before Governor Festus and King Agrippa (Acts 26).

Knowing the significance of witnesses, Paul gives a partial list of persons, including the apostles, who had seen the risen Lord and adds, "Then last of all He was seen by me also, as by one born out of due time" (1 Corinthians 15:3-8). His expression, "as one born out of due time," means he was not chosen to be a witness in the usual order of things. He recognized that those who had followed from Galilee were the first witnesses (Acts 13:31). They had seen Jesus during the 40 days before He ascended. Only a few people had been allowed this privilege and only 12 had been commissioned to be apostles. Paul's case was unique in that Jesus' appearance to him was not until five or six years after the Lord's ascension. He was "last of all," the last so commissioned.

In every instance, the first eyewitnesses had not believed until confronted by undeniable evidence. This was not lack of allegiance. They loved Jesus and grieved over His departure, but they did not expect to see Him alive. It was only after Jesus met with them at different times and places that they all could be convinced. He had conversed with them, eaten with them, and allowed them to examine the crucifixion wounds. He also impressed upon them that everything had happened in fulfilment of prophecy. However, not only did Paul not believe in the possibility that Jesus had arisen, he had fanatically dedicated himself in hateful and blasphemous opposition to those who did. We first meet him at the stoning of Stephen (Acts 7:54-60). Then he was the leading force, driving much of the church out of Jerusalem (Acts 8, 26:9-11).

Which three chapters in Acts tell of Paul's conversion?

. . . .

Before Paul, how many others are recorded as having seen the risen Christ?

. . . .

How many had been appointed apostles?

. . . .

How does the cause of Paul's unbelief differ from that of the first witnesses?

The Story

He was on his way to Damascus to continue the persecution when suddenly, about noon, somewhere near the city, there was a light from heaven brighter than the sun. Paul and his companions fell to the ground. Just as Jesus had chosen the times and places to appear to others, He chose this as the time and place for Paul to see His resurrected glory. It was an event forever engraved in his mind.

> "I heard a voice speaking to me and saying in the Hebrew language, 'Saul, Saul, why are you persecuting Me? It is hard for you to kick against the goads.' So I said, 'Who are You, Lord?' And He said, 'I am Jesus, whom you are persecuting'" (Acts 26:14-15).

The metaphor, "kick against the goads," meant that being hostile to Christ was as foolish as an animal that only hurt himself kicking against the sticks, prodding it to move.

It should not be missed that Paul did not instantly assume the vision was Jesus. He had to ask, "Who are You, Lord?" The Lord said, "I am Jesus, whom you are persecuting." It is significant that Jesus identified Himself. One might assume that if Jesus appeared to anyone, He would be easily recognized. Paul certainly knew this was not an ordinary personage, yet he did not recognize Jesus simply by seeing Him. Neither did Christ miraculously implant this knowledge into Paul's brain. Instead, He chose to make Himself known by the spoken word. We can imagine the shock and fear when he realized this was the very Nazarene whose followers he had been determined to destroy (Acts 26:14).

For no other person in the history of the world has there been a like experience. The Lord knows the hearts of all men. He knew the kind of man Paul was. In Paul's own words,

"I was formerly a blasphemer, a persecutor, and an insolent man; but I obtained mercy because I did it ignorantly in unbelief" (1 Timothy 1:13). He was a man of sincere, though misguided, conscience. His unbelief, his unholy fanaticism, was out of ignorance. Prejudice had kept him from the evidence. But the Lord knew that when he saw the truth, he would surrender in faith and obedience. Further, the Lord knew that once convinced, Paul would become a mighty champion for the cause. Thus, He saw in Paul a "chosen vessel" and intervened to make him a witness "born out of due time."

Blinded by the glory of Christ's appearance, Paul was led into the city to await further instructions. Not knowing what else to do, and under the burden of the enormity of his sins, he fasted and prayed. For three days, his tormented conscience waited for an answer. What could be done about his guilt? What was to be his future? Then, on the third day, Ananias, one of the Lord's people in Damascus, was sent to Paul to restore his sight and to tell what was yet required for cleansing from sin. Just as Jesus had promised, Ananias had been sent to tell Paul what he "must do."

> "For you will be His witness to all men of what you have seen and heard. And now why are you waiting? Arise and be baptized, and wash away your sins, calling on the name of the Lord" (Acts 22:15-16).

Though it shocked him into submission, the power that saved him was not the vision itself. As with all others, the power to save is the blood of Christ, made known by the gospel (Romans 1:16). His sins were washed away when, as a penitent believer, he was baptized calling on the name of the Lord. Because God is always consistent with Himself, Paul's case did not set aside the universally required plan of salvation. We cannot suppose that the Lord had decided the gospel plan was not suitable for a sinner like Paul and that, therefore, in his case he made an exception. The Lord is not a respecter of persons. He does not save some by one means and others by another (Acts 10:35-36). Paul was not saved by simply having a remarkable experience. He became a believer when he was convinced of the truth. His repentance was evident, and upon hearing the command to be baptized, he obeyed immediately. Only then were his sins washed away.

> *Did he immediately recognize Jesus when he saw and heard Him?*
>
> . . . .
>
> *What did Christ know about Paul that He would say he was a "chosen vessel?*
>
> . . . .
>
> *Why did he fast and pray for three days?*
>
> . . . .
>
> *What was he told to do about his sins?*

Purpose Stated

If seeing Jesus was not a mere shortcut to make him a believer, what was Christ's purpose in the vision? As was the case with the others, it was necessary for Paul to actually see Christ to be able to be commissioned as an apostolic witness. We remember Peter's explanation that witnesses had to be specifically chosen (Acts 10:40-42). That this was the purpose of this unique miracle is made clear by the express statements of Scripture. Jesus appeared to Paul because He chose him for a special purpose, just as He had chosen Peter, James, John, et al. In the Lord's own words:

"I am Jesus, whom you are persecuting. But rise and stand on your feet; for I have appeared to you for this purpose, to make you a minister and a witness both of the things which you have seen and of the things which I will yet reveal to you. I will deliver you from the Jewish people, as well as from the Gentiles, to whom I now send you, to open their eyes, in order to turn them from darkness to light, and from the power of Satan to God, that they may receive forgiveness of sins and an inheritance among those who are sanctified by faith in Me" (Acts 26:15-18).

Before Ananias was sent to see Paul in Damascus, the Lord had given the same explanation to him. "He is a chosen vessel of Mine to bear My name before Gentiles, kings, and the children of Israel" (Acts 9:15). Thus, as instructed, Ananias said,

"The God of our fathers has chosen you that you should know His will, and see the Just One, and hear the voice of His mouth. For you will be His witness to all men of what you have seen and heard" (Acts 22:14-15).

What was the stated purpose of Jesus appearing to Paul?

. . . .

What is the significance of his being "last of all"?

Compelling Court Testimony (Acts 26)

Because he now preached the faith he once sought to destroy, Paul, the persecutor, became one of the persecuted. His zeal for Christ brought upon him the murderous hostility of the Jewish hierarchy, and this had forced him into the protection and custody of the Roman authorities. He was taken to Caesarea for trial, first before governor Felix and later in the court of Festus. Though Festus found no basis for charges against Paul, the apostle knew the governor wanted to appease the Jews. Uncertain, therefore, as to the integrity and reliability of the provincial government, he had asserted his rights as a Roman citizen and appealed to Caesar.

While Paul was awaiting transportation to Rome, King Agrippa visited Festus and learned of the situation. A public hearing was arranged that Agrippa might hear the case himself. Unlike Festus, whose concerns were only secular and political, Agrippa, having been reared in the Jewish religion, was already familiar with the issues between Christians and Jews. Paul would use the occasion, not only to defend himself, but especially to persuade Agrippa to become a Christian.

The prominence of the apostle's case drew an impressive gallery of dignitaries, including chief captains and leading men of the city. This would be no ordinary tribunal. Regardless of what they may have expected to hear, rather than a supposed criminal trying to vindicate himself, they would, in fact, hear a powerful and irrefutable apology for the Christian religion.

At the appointed time, Agrippa and his sister, Bernice, came with pomp and ceremony to take their place in the chamber. Festus opened the proceedings and gave leave to Paul to speak for himself. The great apostle stretched forth his hand in a gesture of bold confidence and recounted his life story. The record was beyond dispute. His early religious devotion as a Pharisee and his sincerity and zeal as a persecutor of Christians were well-known. There had been complete reversal, of course, and now his Jewish enemies sought to kill him for preaching the very things that their own prophets had foretold, i.e., "that the Christ would suffer, that He would be the first to rise from the dead, and would proclaim light to the Jewish people and to the Gentiles" (v. 23). It could only be explained by the experience on the Damascus road.

Upon hearing Paul speak of Christ rising from the dead, Festus lost his composure, shouting with a loud voice: "Paul, you are beside yourself! Much learning is driving you mad" (v. 24). It is not surprising that this Gentile, reacting from a heathen world-view, would be so astounded that a man like Paul could believe the dead could arise. All heathen cultures have notions of some kind of afterlife, but only Christians base their hope on the fact that their Founder's dead and buried corpse arose to live forever. Doubtless confused by the twists in Paul's story and his assertion that a dead person had come back to life, Festus had no better response than to say Paul was suffering delusion.

However, the details of Paul's defense were hardly the ravings of a mentally disturbed man. Each element in the sequence of events as Paul recounted them was public knowledge and beyond dispute except for his claim that he had seen Jesus. That, however, was the lynchpin that held it all together. Without it, Paul's remarkable life could not be explained. The court had Paul's declaration that he had seen Christ. Only if the vision were true, could the rest make sense. On what legal basis could his testimony be rejected? The Roman governor was astounded by what he heard, but made no charge of perjury. If Paul were perjuring himself, there could have been serious consequences. Yet the judges, Festus and Agrippa, found no criminal fault in his testimony? (Acts 26:31-32).

> *What was the only point in his testimony that was not admittedly public knowledge?*
>
> . . . .
>
> *Why do so many cultures believe in an afterlife, but not in a bodily resurrection?*

Another Credible Witness

The same criteria that assured the credibility of the earlier witnesses can be applied to Paul. As with them, his competence is obvious. Not only in the speech before Festus and Agrippa, but in all his speaking and writing, he is a rational and educated intellectual. Neither is there any hearsay in his testimony, only first-hand knowledge of what (Who) he saw and heard. Though not part of the original group, there is perfect consistency with their testimony. Paul had seen Jesus in totally isolated circumstances, but his testimony was the same as their testimony: Jesus is risen, Jesus is alive. As to reliability, what man would have endured so much, even under threat of death, had he not been certain his testimony was absolute truth?

> "Paul's case was unique in that Jesus' appearance to him was not until five or six years after the Lord's ascension. He was 'last of all,' the last so commissioned."

Especially to be considered in Paul's case is whether he had preconceived expectations, or biases, which would have affected what he said he witnessed. As had been seen in the cases of the first witnesses, he had no expectation ever to see Jesus alive. In their case, either they had forgotten or had never comprehended Christ's repeated assurances. It was not a lack of love and loyalty on their part, only weakness of faith. In Paul's case, however, his refusal to believe had been compounded by his hatred of the very name of Jesus.

There is special significance in favor of his credibility, therefore, in the remarkable transformation that took place in his life. In this respect, no other testimony compares to his case.

It was more than a change of convictions, or even the embracing of a new worldview. It was the acceptance of a radically different life, one that meant brutal hardships, imprisonment, and eventually death, all because he was absolutely certain he had seen the Christ.

Many Bible scholars have thought that Paul's story by itself proves Christ's resurrection. The change in his life and his dedication to the Christian cause cannot be explained without the Damascus road experience. History is history. No one should imagine that the sacred historian invented Paul. There is too much evidence of Paul's influence in the first-century world. The question is not whether Paul's conversion can be proven as history, but whether his conversion is proof of the resurrection. There is no other explanation.

How does Paul meet all the criteria of a credible witness?

. . . .

What is it about Paul's history that makes his claim to have seen Jesus so compelling?

. . . .

Why is it unreasonable for anyone to dismiss his story as fiction?

. . . .

Why might Festus and other unbelievers suggest that he and other witnesses suffered from delusions?

CHAPTER TWELVE

Christ the Firstfruits

IT IS NOT NECESSARY TO ARGUE FROM SCRIPTURE THE inevitability of death and its seeming finality. The texts that declare man's corporeal mortality only serve as sobering reminders of what everyone knows. Solomon's observations about all earthly pursuits always end the same way. "For what happens to the sons of men also happens to animals; one thing befalls them: as one dies, so dies the other. Surely, they all have one breath; man has no advantage over animals, for all is vanity. All go to one place: all are from the dust, and all return to dust" (Ecclesiastes 3:19-20). Our fleshly bodies are destined to die and decay.

In death the spirit, the inner person, separates from the body. "The body without the spirit is dead" (James 2:26). But the spirit that leaves the body is not dead. "Then shall the dust return to the earth as it was: and the spirit shall return unto God who gave it" (Ecclesiastes 12:7). As Jesus was dying, He prayed, "Father, into Your hands I commit My spirit" (Luke 23:46). He knew His spirit would leave His body. A short time before, He told the penitent robber, "Assuredly, I say to you, today you will be with Me in Paradise" (Luke 23:43). That very day both Jesus and the robber died. Their spirits left their bodies and both went to paradise. We know this does not mean they went to heaven because on the day of His resurrection Jesus told Mary, "I have not yet ascended to My Father" (John 20:17).

There is an intermediate place wherein are held the spirits of the dead until the resurrection. It is called "hades," meaning a place that cannot be seen. Jesus was in Hades while His body was in the tomb (Acts 2:31). For the righteous, hades is a place of comfort/paradise. For the unrighteous, it is a place of torment.

In His account of the selfish rich man and poor Lazarus, Jesus described how one was in comfort and the other was in torment. In both cases their bodies were dead, but they were in a state of consciousness (Luke 16:19-31). The spirits of those who were disobedient are in "prison" (1 Peter 3:19-20). Those who die "in the Lord" are blessed because they rest from their labors (Revelation 14:13).

Christians are in one sense with Jesus in this life. In another sense, the spirits of the righteous will be with Christ while awaiting the resurrection. Paul foresaw that for him to die would be to "gain," because in departing this life he would go to "be with Christ, which is far better" (Philippians 1:21-23). In another place he wrote,

Are the spirits of the dead conscious?

. . . .

While Jesus' body was in the grave, was His spirit in hades?

Was His spirit in paradise? Is this the same as heaven?

. . . .

Is there a place for the spirits of the unrighteous dead?

So we are always confident, knowing that while we are at home in the body we are absent from the Lord. For we walk by faith, not by sight. (2 Corinthians 5:6-7).

What about the Body?

It may seem easier to believe in a spirit existence after death than to believe a dead and decomposing body can be brought back to life. Various non-Christian religions hold to some view of the soul/spirit's existence in the afterlife. Even agnostics might like to think that the deceased are somewhere "up there." Christians have the Bible's assurance that there is a good place for us when we leave our bodies in death. However, that isn't all God has in store. The Bible also assures that there is something yet for our bodies. At the second coming of Christ, our bodies will be reunited with our spirits and made alive forever. The Bible's promise is not for an eternal home for disembodied spirits. Rather, heaven is for bodies resurrected and made immortal.

If we rely only on earthly observations, a resurrection of the body seems impossible. Many objections can be offered. The flesh decomposes. Some corpses are consumed by fire, some lost at sea, some consumed by animals, etc. Some die in infancy, some in their prime, and others in old age. To believe the spirit has gone to heaven seems easier to comprehend than that a corpse we have watched buried into the ground will someday be restored to life. Only by the assurances of Scripture can we hope for "the redemption of our bodies" (Romans 8:23). Only God can make it possible. "For with God nothing will be impossible" (Luke 1:37).

Paul asked King Agrippa, "Why should it be thought incredible by you that God raises the dead?" (Acts 26:8).

Confidence in the resurrection begins with our belief in God as Almighty. "God both raised up the Lord and will also raise us up by His power" (1 Corinthians 6:14).

Does the Bible promise that our bodies will be brought back to life?

. . . .

Is heaven a place for disembodied spirits?

General Resurrection (John 5:28-29; Acts 24:15)

At the Second Coming of Christ, there will be a day of Judgment and all will be there (2 Corinthians 5:10; Revelation 20:11-15). It will not be to ascertain guilt or innocence. Every man's record is already known. The spirits of the righteous dead are now "blessed" and "rest from their labors" (Revelation 14:13). The spirits of the disobedient are held in "prison" (1 Peter 3:19-20).

In the resurrection, the spirits of the dead will be reunited with their bodies, and all the dead will be raised. There will be "a resurrection of the dead, both of the just and the unjust" (Acts 24:15).

The prophet Daniel affirmed, "And many of those who sleep in the dust of the earth shall awake, Some to everlasting life, Some to shame and everlasting contempt" (Daniel 12:2). Jesus was specific in declaring the same.

> Do not marvel at this; for the hour is coming in which
> all who are in the graves will hear His voice and come
> forth — those who have done good, to the resur-
> rection of life, and those who have done evil, to the
> resurrection of condemnation (John 5:28-29).

Then will be vindicated the righteous justice of God, "who will render to each one according to his deeds" (Romans 2:7). Jesus described the separate destinies of the resurrected dead who stand before the Judge. "And these will go away into everlasting punishment, but the righteous into eternal life" (Matthew 25:46). God "is able to destroy both soul and body in hell" (Matthew 10:28).

It may be questioned why all the dead will be raised at the same time. It is expected that the Scriptures would give greater attention to the resurrection of the righteous, but it is no less certain that the ungodly will also be raised. There is much we may not understand about the purposes of God. We know, however, that beginning with our first ancestor, death became the lot of all humanity (Romans 5:12-15). In the righteous justice of God, therefore, it is determined that all lost by Adam's sin is to be regained by Christ's righteousness. "For since by man came death, by Man also came the resurrection of the dead. For as in Adam all die, even so in Christ all shall be made alive" (1 Corinthians 15:21-22).

Will all the dead be raised at the same time?

. . . .

What are that only possible destinies after the Judgment?

Our Hope (1 Thessalonians 4:13-18)

Immature Christians at Thessalonica needed assurance concerning those who would be in their graves at the time of Christ's Second Coming. Would those who "sleep in Jesus" be left behind? Paul assuaged their concerns with a brief outline of the Divine plan.

> But I do not want you to be ignorant, brethren, concerning those who have fallen asleep, lest you sorrow as others who have no hope. For if we believe that Jesus died and rose again, even so God will bring with Him those who sleep in Jesus.

Sleep is a metaphor for being dead based on the corpse appearing to be asleep. Christians can have hope for being brought back to life because we believe that Jesus died and was brought back to life.

We can be confident that God will bring us back by the same power that brought Jesus back. "He who raised up the Lord Jesus will also raise us up with Jesus, and will present us with you" (2 Corinthians 4:14). The meaning is not, as some have supposed, that God will bring the spirits of the dead back from heaven. Rather, it is about bringing the dead from their graves.

"Christians have the Bible's assurance that there is a good place for us when we leave our bodies in death. However, that isn't all God has in store."

The Thessalonians (and all Christians) can be assured, therefore, that when Jesus comes again the dead in Christ will not be left behind.

For this we say to you by the word of the Lord, that we who are alive and remain until the coming of the Lord will by no means precede those who are asleep. For the Lord Himself will descend from heaven with a shout, with the voice of an archangel, and with the trumpet of God. And the dead in Christ will rise first. Then we who are alive and remain shall be caught up together with them in the clouds to meet the Lord in the air. And thus we shall always be with the Lord. Therefore comfort one another with these words (1 Thessalonians 4:15-18).

What seems to have been especially of concern for the Thessalonians about the dead?

. . . .

What is meant by the statement "And the dead in Christ will rise first"?

Before the living saints ascend to meet the Lord in the air, the dead will be raised so that all can go together to be with the Lord forever. This corresponds with the wonderful promise made in John 14:1-3. Jesus said, "I will come again and receive you to Myself; that where I am, there you may be also."

Christ the Firstfruits (1 Corinthians 15:20-26)

In his great chapter on the resurrection, Paul spoke of Jesus as the "firstfruits" of the resurrection. The metaphor comes from the Old Testament, which required the firstfruits of the harvest to be offered to the Lord (Leviticus 23:10-11). This acknowledged that what was produced was from God. It also trusted that the rest of the harvest would follow. The figure is applied to Christ as the first to arise and ascend, so the rest will follow (1 Corinthians 15:20-23).

At Corinth some were denying the possibility of the dead being raised. As with most people, they could not conceive how a body once returned to the earth could ever live again. Paul replies with several points, especially emphasizing that Jesus Himself was a man in the flesh. He died and had been raised. If, therefore, Christ was raised, resurrection is possible. "But each one in his own order: Christ the firstfruits, afterward those who are Christ's at His coming." A similar expression, "firstborn from the dead," emphasizes His preeminence (Colossians 1:18).

The story of the resurrection is about a real man. He is more than a man, but He is a man. As a man He died and was buried. The dead man Jesus came back to life. Until then, there was no basis by which men and women might face death without dread. Because Jesus became one of us in the flesh and in death, His resurrection assures us of our own. Hebrews 2:14-15 explains,

> "Inasmuch then as the children have partaken of flesh and blood, He Himself likewise shared in the same, that through death He might destroy him who had the power of death, that is, the devil, and release those who through fear of death were all their lifetime subject to bondage."

In what sense is the metaphor "firstfruits" applied to Jesus?

What had kept people in bondage all their lives?

What does it mean that Christ had "partaken of flesh and blood" and does the text emphasize this?

What Kind of Body? (1 Corinthians 15:35-58)

"But someone will say, "How are the dead raised? And with what kind of body do they come?" Paul's blunt reply ("Foolish one") shows that such was the scoffing question of an unbeliever. It is foolish to think God cannot provide what He promises. One need only to consider the world around us to know that God is able to provide a suitable body for the resurrected dead.

- Seed dies in the ground and comes up alive as a new body, yet of the same kind. It is God who "gives it a body as He pleases, and to each seed its own body" (vv. 36-38).

- The God who made the many varieties of flesh bodies, the God who made the varieties that compose the universe — He is the God who will provide the resurrection body (vv. 39-41).

- Paul continues the analogy of seed. In death the body is sown in corruption, raised in incorruption; sown in dishonor, raised in glory; sown in weakness, raised in power, sown a natural body, raised a spiritual body (vv. 42-44).

The thing to know about the body to be resurrected is that there is a "natural body" and a "spiritual body." We know that our natural bodies came from Adam. The spiritual body, however, will come by Christ. As the "first man," Adam was the progenitor of earthly life, so Christ is figuratively called "the last Adam" because by Him we will have a spiritual body.

> However, the spiritual is not first, but the natural,
> and afterward the spiritual. The first man was of the
> earth, made of dust; the second Man is the Lord
> from heaven. As was the man of dust, so also are
> those who are made of dust; and as is the heavenly
> Man, so also are those who are heavenly. And as we
> have borne the image of the man of dust, we shall
> also bear the image of the heavenly Man (vv. 45-49).

Jesus is the "heavenly man." He did not ascend into heaven as a disembodied spirit, but as "the Man Christ Jesus" (1 Timothy 2:5). The plain declaration is that as surely as that in our present life we have the likeness (fleshly body) of Adam, so in the resurrection we will have the likeness of Christ.

> For our citizenship is in heaven, from which we also
> eagerly wait for the Savior, the Lord Jesus Christ,
> who will transform our lowly body that it may be
> conformed to His glorious body, according to the
> working by which He is able even to subdue all
> things to Himself (Philippians 3:20-21).

The "lowly body" we inhabit now will be changed into a "glorious body." This seemingly impossible change is in fact absolutely possible, because all things are possible with God. Further, the change is no less certain for Christians who are alive, yet in the natural body.

> Behold, I tell you a mystery: We shall not all sleep, but
> we shall all be changed — in a moment, in the twin-
> kling of an eye, at the last trumpet. For the trumpet

> will sound, and the dead will be raised incorruptible,
> and we shall be changed. For this corruptible must put
> on incorruption, and this mortal must put on immortality.
> So when this corruptible has put on incorruption,
> and this mortal has put on immortality, then shall be
> brought to pass the saying that is written: "Death is
> swallowed up in victory" (vv. 51-54).

Clearly, in the resurrection that which is "mortal," the body, must put on "immortality. Only then will there be total victory over death.

With regard to our bodies, how are Adam and Jesus compared?

. . . .

Is Jesus' body in heaven? How is His body different from a flesh and blood body?

. . . .

What are the several adjectives applied to what our spiritual bodies will be?

. . . .

What will happen to Christians who are alive when Jesus comes?

In our present earthly state, we are unable to visualize a body that is "spiritual," "glorious," incorruptible," and "heavenly." One who denies this must assume he knows everything and that nothing can exist which he cannot understand. Christians know that God can do more than we can even imagine (Ephesians 3:20). God promises we will have a body like the glorious body of Jesus.

> "Beloved, now we are
> children of God; and
> it has not yet been
> revealed what we shall
> be, but we know that
> when He is revealed,
> we shall be like Him,
> for we shall see Him
> as He is" (1 John 3:2).

Will We Know One Another?

Why would it be supposed that a spiritual body would have no personal identity? We will know Jesus. We will "see Him as He is." When He ascended beyond the clouds and entered heaven, He took on His glorious body. He did not, however, change His identity. He is the same Jesus the apostles saw going away and will be the same Jesus when He comes again. We do not know how we will recognize Him, but we are assured that we will "see Him as He is." In that "we shall be like Him," does it not follow that if He has features that identify Him, should not we also? Such was the confidence of Job.

> For I know that my Redeemer lives, And He shall stand
> at last on the earth; And after my skin is destroyed,
> this I know, That in my flesh I shall see God, Whom
> I shall see for myself, And my eyes shall behold, and
> not another (Job 19:25-27a).

We might also consider whether we will know ourselves. Such seems a foolish question, for if one does not know himself, how would he know he is there? How would he know he had received his inheritance?

If in heaven it will not be possible to recognize one another, how will we know whether our friends and loved ones are there? Would that not mean being deprived of one of the most attractive hopes we have regarding eternal life?

To the Corinthians, Paul spoke of "knowing that he who raised the Lord Jesus will raise us also with Jesus and bring us with you into his presence" (2 Corinthians 4:14, ESV). To hope to be with them would seem meaningless if they would not know one another.

Several references to persons dying speak of their being "gathered to his people, "go to your fathers," or "gathered to their fathers" (Genesis 25:8, 17; 15:15; Judges 2:10). This was not in reference to their going to common graves because some were buried in distant places.

> "Because Jesus became one of us in the flesh and in death, His resurrection assures us of our own."

David's question upon learning of the death of his infant child strongly implies his expectation to be reunited with him in another world. "But now he is dead; why should I fast? Can I bring him back again? I shall go to him, but he shall not return to me" (2 Samuel 12:23).

To the Thessalonians, Paul wrote, "But we, brethren, having been taken away from you for a short time in presence, not in heart, endeavored more eagerly to see your face with great desire. Therefore we wanted to come to you — even I, Paul, time and again — but Satan hindered us."

He wanted to see them face to face, but it had not been possible. However, they would be together at Christ's coming. "For what is our hope, or joy, or crown of rejoicing? Is it not even you in the presence of our Lord Jesus Christ at His coming? For you are our glory and joy" (1 Thessalonians 2:17-20).

Paul assured the Thessalonians that the resurrected dead and the living would be "caught up together" to meet the Lord. If the saved cannot recognize one another, why would "together" be any better than separate? *Together* implies being reunited. Part of that eternal togetherness even includes companionship with saints from ages past. Jesus said, "And I say to you that many will come from east and west, and sit down with Abraham, Isaac, and Jacob in the kingdom of heaven" (Matthew 8:11).

Would it make sense for persons in heaven to not know themselves?

. . . .

What Old Testament examples seem to imply knowing one another in heaven?

. . . .

What was Paul's hope about being in the presence of Christ with those saints to whom he wrote?

www.ingramcontent.com/pod-product-compliance
Lightning Source LLC
Chambersburg PA
CBHW051426090426
42737CB00014B/2847